# ANCIENT GREECE IN FIFTY MONUMENTS

DAVID STUTTARD

# ANCIENT GREECE IN · FIFTY MONUMENTS

T&H

# CONTENTS

INTRODUCTION

# BUILDING THE GREEK WORLD

IT WAS A GREEK who first identified the world's greatest monuments. Of his seven choices, Antipater of Sidon, a poet whose life straddled the second and first centuries BC, was magnanimous enough to include three that had been built by non-Greek speakers (though, when he wrote, the lands that they were in were ruled by Greeks): Egypt's pyramids of Giza, Babylon's walls and Babylon's gardens. Three others were pure Greek: the statue of Zeus at Olympia, on Greece's mainland; the colossal statue of the sun god Helios astride the harbour mouth at Rhodes; and the Temple of Artemis, which Antipater said 'soared up to the clouds', the most awe-inspiring sight under the sun ('apart from Mount Olympus'), in Ephesus on what is now the Turkish coast. The seventh was a hybrid, the tomb of Mausolus at Halicarnassus, built for a Carian king by Greek architects. Another Greek essentially agreed, though in his *Seven Wonders of the World* he substituted for the walls of Babylon the lighthouse at the entrance to the port of Alexandria, a Greek city in Egypt founded by a Greek. This book is credited to Philo of Byzantium, but since two men bore that name – a third-century BC engineer and a fourth-century AD writer of paradoxes – we do not know if it precedes Antipater's or is later.

Both lists, however, are instructive. All the monuments displayed impressive engineering or design (the hydraulics of Babylon's hanging gardens, whatever these may have been, still baffle scientists today), and, constructed over three millennia, most were distinguished for their size. Some served a practical purpose (the Colossus of Rhodes and Pharos of Alexandria both guided sailors into port; the city walls protected Babylon); others (the pyramids and Mausoleum) were funerary monuments; and others were religious (the Temple of Artemis at Ephesus and statue of Zeus at Olympia). All were undoubtedly breathtaking. Writing in Nikopolis on the yawning Bay of Actium in the second century AD, the Greek philosopher Epictetus observed, 'you journey to Olympia to gaze upon the statue of Zeus, and every one of you would consider it a great misfortune to die without ever seeing it.' Later shipped to Constantinople, the statue was destroyed by fire in AD 462. Shortly afterwards, the building in which it once stood was toppled in an earthquake. Artemis' temple and Mausolus' tomb likewise fell into ruins. Of the other wondrous monuments, only the pyramids survive, and even they have been long stripped of their original white limestone façades. But the lists of Philo and Antipater remain, and they are inspirational, for not only do they confirm the great significance that Greeks placed in their

**'THE MONUMENTS AROSE, TOWERING AND INCOMPARABLE IN FORM AND BEAUTY.'**

PLUTARCH
*Life of Pericles*

buildings and their statues, but they remind us, too, of the place their monuments once held in the imagination, of what they meant to those who first commissioned them, then built and used them, and of how today they help to tell those people's story and the wider history of Greece.

In this book we consider fifty such monuments. They range in time from around 1600 BC, when the Aegean island of Thera (modern Santorini) was home to a thriving maritime community, and a Cretan king ruled from his palace at Knossos, through the era of the legendary Trojan War, the Archaic Age, which saw Greece begin to redefine its culture following a catastrophic collapse, the Classical and Hellenistic periods, when most of the now iconic monuments such as the Parthenon were built, and up to 31 BC, when at Actium (where Epictetus was to live two centuries later) Rome's soon-to-be Emperor Augustus erected a memorial commemorating victory over Cleopatra, not just the queen of Egypt but the last surviving independent ruler who was Greek.

Geographically, too, the book is wide-ranging, since the Greek world was not confined to the Greek mainland and Aegean islands. From the eighth century BC onwards, young men sailed in black ships west to Sicily and Italy, south to North Africa and east to the coasts of Asia Minor (now Anatolia in modern Turkey) and the Black Sea to found new cities and export Greek culture to new lands. Even before this diaspora, Greeks had been ethnically diverse: Ionians and Dorians, Aeolians, Achaeans, each with their own dialects and rituals. In the Classical and Hellenistic periods, they had many different constitutions. Often, they waged war on one another. But uniting them throughout the centuries was, in the words of their first historian, Herodotus, 'a kinship in blood and speech, the shrines of gods, the sacrifices that we have in common, and the likeness of our way of life.'

Greece, then, was not a place but an idea. Greeks were still Greeks, no matter if they lived in Syracuse or Sparta or Sinope, and they used many of their monuments as hymns to their Greek way of life and to promote their cultural identity. The design and decoration of their temples, council offices and theatres, the character of the memorials they raised to mark significant events, the way they housed their dead, the legends that grew up around their buildings and their landscapes: all these give evidence of the men and women whose shifting and developing ideas – be they social, political or religious – helped shape the Greek world and in turn helped shape our own.

None of us will gaze with our own eyes upon the statue of Zeus at Olympia, but thanks to the painstaking work of modern artists and their reconstructions we can again experience something of its visual grandeur, and of all the monuments covered in this book. Philo and Antipater chose just seven. We have the luxury of fifty. Each contributes to our understanding, and remains of all of them can still be visited today. And while some can seem at first sight to be little but a heap of rubble, that very rubble can help build a picture of how structures looked, how they were used, how they in turn were part of the experience of being Greek. So, it is to a landscape not of ruins but of gleaming marble, sharp-cut stone and vibrant colours that we travel now to experience the world of ancient Greece through fifty of its most important monuments.

An imaginative reconstruction of the statue of Zeus at Olympia by French artist Antoine-Chrysostôme Quatremère de Quincy gives a good idea of its size but wrongly places it beneath a vaulted ceiling.

# I.

# THE BRONZE AGE

# BEGINNINGS

(*c.* 1600–*c.* 1050 BC)

FOR MOST BRONZE AGE GREEKS, the sea was their life blood. The mainland's mountainous interior meant that travel overland was difficult. So, towns grew up by sheltered shores, where boats could anchor or be dragged onto the beach. Merchants criss-crossed the archipelago of the Aegean, while some struck south to Libya and Egypt or east to the long coast of Asia Minor or even through the racing Hellespont to the Black Sea. People from these lands were sailing too, and by 1600 BC there were already long-established trade routes, which saw not only goods exchanged, but ideas.

Almost midway between mainland Greece, Crete and Asia Minor, the conical island of Thera was perfectly located. Not just an important entrepot, it was a busy processing centre for Cypriot copper, and its economy and cultural life were booming. Among its towns was one that nestled on its southern slopes above a harbour, narrow streets radiating from a triangular piazza, houses cheek-by-jowl with temples. Close to the quayside, one of these, now called prosaically Xeste 3, was a three-storeyed building with fifteen rooms on each of its two lower floors. Faced in well-cut blocks of tufa it had a paved vestibule with stone benches on either side, its walls painted with life-sized images of young men, one capturing a bull, another grasping the horns of a yellow goat as he leaps over its back. Next came a room with forest scenes – palm trees; a lion attacking a small antelope; a blue duck; a red dragonfly – while another room, home to a lustral basin (a sunken area possibly used for ritual purification), showed images of women making offerings and dancing. Elsewhere on this ground floor were scenes of young men, shaven headed, bringing sacred objects to an older seated man dressed in

**'THEY LOVED WAR AND VIOLENCE. THEIR TOOLS WERE OF BRONZE; THEIR HOMES WERE OF BRONZE; THEIR WORK WAS ALL IN BRONZE.'**

HESIOD
*Works & Days*

Called today 'The Saffron Gatherers', this fresco from the first floor of Xeste 3 dates to the seventeenth century BC.

a pure white loincloth. Back in the vestibule, a staircase, its walls adorned with scenes of flowers and trees in blossom, led up to other rooms, no less magnificently painted. Here there were scenes of swallows swooping on red dragonflies, blue monkeys dancing or strumming stringed instruments, women picking yellow saffron flowers. But central to them all was the goddess known as Potnia, the mistress of nature, enthroned on a stepped platform with a winged griffin at her side. We no longer know what rituals, if any, were performed in Xeste 3, but the exuberance of its art is undeniable.

Nor was Xeste 3 unique. There was no building that did not boast at least one wall painting. Although not especially large, one, now known as the **West House**, was so elaborately decorated that its owners seem to have intended to use its walls deliberately to monumentalize their world. Its lower floor was a maze of storerooms and workshops, including one where flour

was ground. Upstairs, however, was a different story. Here on the walls of one large airy room with windows on two sides, was a fresco of a fisherman as well as a detailed scene, 6 m (20 ft) long: a flotilla of eight boats, hulls dazzlingly painted with birds or running lions, masts garlanded with flowers, oars beating rhythmically as they slice through the dolphin-dancing sea between two towns, their buildings picked out in painstaking detail; men crowding the quayside, people standing on the flat roofs of their homes; and on the wooded hills above them three stags race in terror from a lion. Again, the significance of the fresco eludes us. It may show a religious festival in which boats sailed around the island or perhaps came to Thera from other islands such as Crete. But no matter that we do not know exactly what it shows: it is a monument to Thera's intimate relationship with the sea, the element on which it built its wealth.

That the island was wealthy is undeniable. Its houses were stone built; their rooms were large; their walls were reinforced with wooden beams shipped in from Crete. They even had indoor lavatories: one small room in the West House is equipped with what appears to be a toilet, though some have argued that its piping was installed for ritual purposes. The town was certainly equipped with a sophisticated drainage system. But

Opposite and above: Wall paintings from the West House offer vivid snapshots of life on Santorini in the mid-second millennium BC.

Below: A gold Minoan ring (today known as the Ring of Minos) from the fifteenth century BC appears to show the epiphany of a goddess at a rural shrine.

despite its riches – its imported pottery, its bathtubs and its braziers, its beehives, its well-crafted furniture – nothing could save Thera. Unbeknownst to its inhabitants, they were living on the slopes of an active volcano, and around 1620 BC, after days or weeks of tremors which allowed them to escape (as evidenced by the lack of associated human remains), almost the entire island exploded. Whether they reached safety is another question. The massive eruption, unleashing well over 1,000 megatons of energy, caused waves 18 m (60 ft) high. No ships could have survived. The sea would have swamped them. As for our town on the southern coast, its streets and houses with their vivid frescoes were frozen in time, buried under layers of ash and pumice.

Happily for Crete, 150 km (93 miles) south, the tsunami did not engulf its coastal towns, such as the one painstakingly engraved onto a signet ring two centuries later, its impression now preserved in clay. It shows a rocky shoreline, above which nestles a profusion of close-packed multi-storeyed buildings with tall doors and windows, their flat roofs crowned with 'horns of consecration' (architectural ornaments suggestive of the horns of sacred bulls) and, towering above everything, a male figure many times life-sized, holding a spear or sceptre in his outstretched right hand. He may be a god. Another signet ring appears to show two goddesses: one seated in a seaside landscape dotted with enclosures, while male worshippers pluck fruit to offer her; another piloting a boat with an elegant duck's-head prow and, on its deck, an altar crowned with 'horns of consecration'. This delicate gold artefact, just 1.65 cm (⅔ in.) in diameter, is called today the Ring of Minos after the legendary king who gives his name ('Minoan') to this period of Crete's Bronze Age culture and was said to rule from Knossos – according to the Greek historian, Thucydides, the first thalassocracy (or sea-based empire).

Nestling in a fertile plain below the sacred peak of Mount Iuktas with its sanctuary to the sky god, later identified as Zeus, the sprawling **Palace at Knossos** – some 20,000 sq. m (215,278 sq. ft) in area – had a long history. Weathering fires and earthquakes, its most impressive iteration was built around 1650 BC. At its heart was a broad central court, 54 × 27 m (177 × 89 ft), the setting for the bull-leaping events that played a major role in Cretan religious life and were celebrated in stucco frescoes and bronze models. This obsession with the bull, a powerful symbol of fertility, gave rise to the myth of the Minotaur. Half-man, half-bull, this creature demanded an annual tribute of young Athenian men and women – until their prince, Theseus, killed it, picking his way back out of its lair, the twisting labyrinth with the help of the Cretan Princess Ariadne. Overcome by love for him, she gave Theseus one end of a ball of wool, which, standing at the entrance to the labyrinth, she gradually unravelled as he penetrated its dark passages. To find his way out, all Theseus

Below: A high-relief fresco from the Palace at Knossos shows a griffin (a mythological creature with a lion's body and eagle's head and wings) chained to a column.

Opposite, above: A reconstruction of the 'Queen's Megaron' at Knossos shows its rich decorations, including fish and leaping dolphins above one of its doors.

Opposite, below: Dating from between 1500 and 1450 BC, a clay vessel from the island of Pseira, off the coast of north-east Crete, is decorated with distinctive double axes.

Overleaf. A reconstruction of the Palace at Knossos gives a clear idea of its dynamic architecture as well as the interplay of public and private areas.

needed to do was follow the wool trail, winding it up again until he could emerge triumphant into the sunlight (a metaphor for overcoming death).

The word 'labyrinth' (literally 'the place of the double axe') derives from *labrys*, the double axe, whose curving blades formed sharply pointed horns, and which were ritually displayed at Knossos. As for the Minotaur's labyrinthine maze, this may have been inspired by the network of staircases, corridors and rooms within the two- and three-storeyed buildings overlooking the palace's great court. On the northern side, there was a mix of storage and state rooms (one with a high-backed throne and low stone benches facing a lustral basin), to the south domestic quarters and more storerooms. As on Thera, images of people, nature and buildings were everywhere. One storage chest was faced with colourful faience plaques showing houses, and vibrant stuccoed walls were painted with a dazzling array of scenes: leaping dolphins; charging bulls; winged and wingless griffins, one collared and chained to a pillar; bare-breasted women with

Opposite: Controversially reconstructed by Sir Arthur Evans in the early twentieth century, the walls of the throne room at Knossos were painted with griffins in a lush landscape.

Below: Just 3 cm (1 ¼ in.) in length, a clay tablet from the eighteenth century BC bears an inscription written in Linear A.

carefully coiffed hair; lines of young men in loincloths and young women in elaborate long dresses, bearing offerings. Processions such as theirs may have wound into Knossos from the north-east, where a broad, low-stepped 'theatral area' provided a fine viewing platform – though this might also be the dancing floor that Homer tells was made by Daedalus, the celebrated architect, for Ariadne.

Though it was the largest, Knossos was not the only Cretan palace. An even more impressive 'theatral area' was located at the **Palace at Phaistos** across the mountains to the south. Situated between town and palace, and apparently intended as a place for audiences to watch religious rituals, this 'theatral area' was flanked to the north by a flight of eight wide steps, some 24 m (79 ft) long, while to the west a broad staircase partly cut into the living rock climbed to a monumental gateway set into the smooth, towering, two-storeyed west façade. From a porch supported by one central column flanked by pilasters, visitors passed through impressive double doors to a three-columned portico and light-well, from where they could continue either up a staircase, skirting through an airy peristyle courtyard, and on along a corridor to the luxuriant and richly painted so-called royal apartments – or by another staircase out into the central courtyard. At 63 × 22.5 m (207 × 74 ft) and divided north to south by a raised processional causeway, this was both longer and narrower than its counterpart at Knossos. To the north were the loggias of the royal apartments, their impressive columned doorway framed by sentry boxes; to the east a matrix of buildings, in some of which were double axes and horns of

'HERE WAS THE PLACE, WHERE YOUNG MEN AND GIRLS DANCED ... AND CROWDS GATHERED IN JOY ROUND THE DANCING-PLACE.'

HOMER
*Iliad*

consecration; and to the west, behind a colonnade supported by a row of wooden pillars, a suite of rooms that may have had religious purposes. This included a complex of what seem to be small chapels, their walls lined with slabs of gypsum, on whose stone benches were placed altars, sacred vessels and female figurines.

As in other Cretan palaces, Phaistos could boast a multiplicity of storerooms housing giant *pithoi* or storage jars, some conveniently sited next to a quern for grinding grain. Although many details of the structure of Minoan society elude us, this speaks to a high degree of careful planning for the future and tight administration. So too may clay tablets found at many sites, written in a script today called Linear A, whose content remains undeciphered. Equally cryptic is the Phaistos disc, discovered in 1908 in buildings east of the royal apartments. Roughly 16.2 cm (6 ½ in.) in diameter and 1.5 cm (⅝ in.) thick, this circular clay object is stamped on both sides with symbols that spiral from the edge into the centre. Narrow incised lines delineate the spirals and also separate what may be words or phrases. For decades, its authenticity was questioned, but the subsequent discovery of similar symbols now suggests

Opposite: Dating from the seventeenth century BC, the clay Phaistos disc with its stamped text is yet to be deciphered,

Right: Found in Phaistos, this fifteenth-century BC *rhyton*, a vessel for decanting liquids often within ritual settings, is decorated with an underwater scene showing argonauts (a type of octopus) floating above rocks.

Overleaf: Viewed from above, the 'theatral area' of the palace complex at Phaistos can be seen clearly to the left, flanked to the right by buildings including the royal apartments.

that it is genuine. Its purpose and message, however, continue to perplex. Whether it is a historical record, an astrological calendar or (the most recent theory) a hymn to two goddesses, Astarte and a pregnant mother-goddess, it can claim to be the world's earliest example of a stamped, or printed, text.

Phaistos, Knossos and other palaces such as Malia (but not Zakros in eastern Crete) seem largely to have lacked defences, suggesting that they had no fear of attack. But around 1450 BC, many were destroyed by fire. While evidence is scant, it seems likely they were overrun by men who sailed from mainland Greece. We know these men as Mycenaeans, named after the settlement and **FORTRESS CITADEL AT MYCENAE** in the north-east Peloponnese, the richest and most powerful of the mainland cities of its time. In contrast to the Cretan palaces, Mycenae's was forbidding. Crouching on a low triangular hill between two rugged mountains, it commanded not just its own town on an adjoining plateau, but the main road south from Corinth and the rest of Greece, the wide plain of the Argolid, and by extension the sea. Here, the citadel, 30,000 sq. m (323,000 sq. ft) in area, descended the steep slopes in terraces to the imposing walls enclosing it on three sides. Only to the south was there no

need for walls – a precipitous cliff face plunged down to the canyon of the River Chavos far below. Built in the mid-fourteenth century BC, when the settlement was already many centuries old, in places the walls were 12 m (40 ft) high and 7.5 m (24 ½ ft) wide. But it was not simply the walls' overall proportions that were disquieting; it was the size of many of the rough-shaped stones from which they were constructed. They were so large that later generations thought the only beings who could have set them there were legendary Cyclopes, one-eyed giants, the workforce of the god Hephaestus.

Especially menacing was the main entrance, funnelling between the circuit wall and, on the right, a specially built bastion, which, should anyone attack, helped turn the narrow court into a killing ground, where defenders could hurl missiles from three sides. Most arresting of all, however, was the gate itself, an almost square entrance – 3.1 m (10 ft) high and 2.95 m (9 ft 8 in.) wide – originally with heavy double doors, its monolithic gateposts topped by a huge lintel – 4.5 × 2.0 × 0.8 m (15 × 6 ½ × 2 ½ ft) estimated to weigh 18 tons. And if the sheer proportions of these materials were not enough to instil awe, above the gate, in the 'relieving triangle', the space created by the corbel vaulting calculated to direct the weight away out from the centre of the lintel and down onto the gateposts to prevent cracking, was a massive limestone slab – 3.3 × 3.9 × 0.7 m (11 ft × 12 ft 9 in. × 2 ft 3 in.) – carved in high relief with a striking scene:

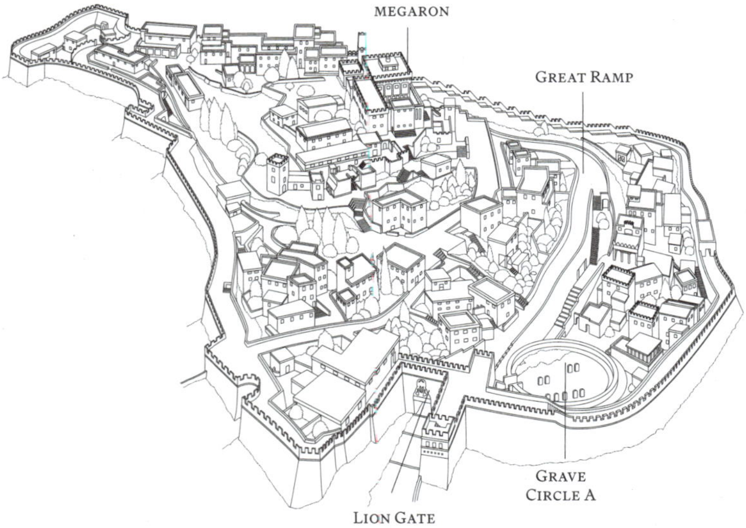

Left: A plan of Mycenae's citadel shows how the Lion Gate led in to a broad avenue that winds up the steep hill towards the royal palace.

Above: This reconstruction of Mycenae around 1250 BC shows townhouses pressing up against the citadel's walls.

at its centre a tall pillar of Minoan design (wider at the top than at the bottom), its base set on two altars, and on either side what seems to be a lioness standing proud, her front paws resting on an altar, her head turned, staring down all comers. Today, both heads are missing. Made of softer stone, much easier to carve, and attached with dowels onto the body, they may already have been lost by the second century AD when the travel writer Pausanias visited. He calls the creatures lions, but it is not impossible that they were griffins, wingless cousins of the chained griffin of Knossos. Lions, though, are probable.

Throughout Greek literature Mycenae's legendary ruler Agamemnon and his brother, Menelaus, are likened to lions, and the image of these creatures guarding the palace is a powerful one. Perhaps the royal family's coat of arms, it is the first truly monumental work of Western art.

Dating from around 1250 BC, the Lion Gate was a century or so younger than the mighty walls, part of a costly building project that saw the fortifications extended in a wide curve to the south-west to include a circle of sixteenth-century BC graves with intricate, carved headstones. This royal cemetery was itself enclosed by a perplexing structure: two parallel circles of sandstone slabs placed vertically, 1.35 m (4 ½ ft) apart, and topped horizontally with other slabs to form a low parapet or wall around 1.5 m (5 ft) high. Entered from a gateway to the north, its purpose is uncertain, but it may have been intended somehow to contain the spirits of those buried in the six graves excavated in the 1870s by Heinrich Schliemann: eight men, nine women and two children. All were buried with expensive gifts and furnishings, including ceremonial swords and daggers, gold cups, gold and silver drinking vessels – one shaped like a bull's

Above: Mycenae's impressive thirteenth-century BC gateway is dominated by twin sculpted lions (or perhaps wingless griffins) flanking a Cretan-style pillar, their front paws on an altar.

Opposite: Found in Mycenae's Grave Circle A, this gold vessel in the shape of a lion's head dates from the sixteenth century BC.

'AS A LION PANICS A HERD OF CATTLE ... JUST SO DID AGAMEMNON FALL ON THE TROJANS.'

HOMER
*Iliad*

head, another like a lion's – rings, necklaces and gems and five gold face masks, one of which Schliemann (wrongly) claimed to show the face of Agamemnon.

From the Lion Gate a (slightly later) ramp ascended past the grave circle and its adjacent religious quarter – a series of shrines and altars, rooms containing statuettes and frescoes showing goddesses and shields – to the royal palace. Here, atop a monumental staircase, an anteroom and lobby gave onto the great hall, or *megaron*, 12.7 m (42 ft 8 in.) long and 11.8 m (38 ft 8 in.) wide, its roof supported by four wooden pillars and, at its centre, a round hearth, 3.4 m (11 ft) in diameter. Painted with glowing frescoes showing women, warriors with chariots and horses, and a battle scene, this was the royal throne room, where the king could entertain and dazzle family, guests and courtiers, display his wealth, project authority and conduct soft diplomacy. According to mythology, that king was Agamemnon, the commander-in-chief of the Greek army at the siege of Troy, who was forced by the gods to sacrifice his daughter to ensure his fleet could sail. In punishment, on his return his wife, Clytemnestra, killed him as he took a bath – and in the private quarters of the

palace, a claustrophobic complex of rooms, corridors and staircases dictated by the unforgiving gradient of the hill on which it stood, a small red stuccoed bathtub still survives.

For Classical Greeks and their successors, Mycenae was inseparable from myth, wherein it was home to a cycle of slaughter and revenge that passed from one generation to the next as the result of a curse placed on the family of Agamemnon's father, Atreus. Legend told how, vying for the throne and for a woman's love, Atreus invited his brother Thyestes to dinner (in Mycenae's *megaron*), pretending that he wanted to be reconciled, but when the meal was finished he revealed what had been eaten: Thyestes' children. The family had a history of such deception: Atreus' grandfather Tantalus once served his own son Pelops at a banquet for the gods. Being divine, when they found out, they reconstructed and resurrected him. Thyestes had no such powers, yet his curse proved inescapable, and even in the second century AD in the landscape round Mycenae's citadel tour guides were claiming that conspicuous monuments were graves of leading members of the ill-fated family.

They named the most conspicuous of all the **Treasury of Atreus**, but this was doubly a misnomer. It was not a treasury, and it did not belong to Atreus. Instead, it was a *tholos* or 'beehive' tomb, one of a number of such constructions that dotted the landscape of Mycenae and wider Bronze Age Greece. All followed roughly the same design: a long passageway, or

Above: The walls of the *megaron* (banqueting hall) of Mycenae's palace were decorated in vivid scenes, such as this one showing warriors, horses and grooms reconstructed in a watercolour.

Opposite: A reconstruction suggests the opulence of the façade of the so-called Treasury of Atreus, the largest of Mycenae's *tholos* tombs dating from the thirteenth century BC.

'HERE ARE THE UNDERGROUND CHAMBERS OF ATREUS AND HIS SONS, THE TREASURE HOUSES OF THEIR WEALTH.'

PAUSANIAS
*Description of Greece*

*dromos*, led to a doorway, which opened into the tomb itself, a round construction with a corbelled roof, originally covered with a mound of earth to add height and visual impact. Its mound is now partially eroded, but the Treasury of Atreus remains impressive. Apart from the addition of a rectangular anteroom, what distinguished it were both its scale and splendour: at 14.5 m (47 ½ ft) in diameter and 13.2 m (43 ft 4 in.) high, its main chamber was the most monumental ever constructed, and to this day its corbelled dome remains the largest in the world. Starting from a wide paved artificial terrace, its *dromos*, 36 m (118 ft) long and 6 m (20 ft) wide), ran from east

Left: Even today, Mycenae's so-called Treasury of Atreus, approached by its long tapering *dromos*, fills visitors with awe.

Below: A detail of one of the pillars from the façade of the Treasury of Atreus shows the swirl pattern typical of Mycenaean art.

Opposite: The corbelled east gallery of the Citadel of Tiryns tunnels through its stout defensive walls.

to west, tunnelling into the natural hillside. It was flanked by ashlar walls, 0.5 m (1 ½ ft) high at the entrance rising steadily to 10 m (33 ft) at the tomb's façade. Here, the doorway – 5.4 m (17 ft 9 in.) tall, 2.7 m (8 ft 10 in.) wide, 5.4 m (17 ft 9 in.) deep – was capped by two enormous lintel stones. One, weighing nigh on 120 tons, is the heaviest block of masonry ever used in an ancient Greek building.

As with the roughly contemporary Lion Gate, the lintel was topped by a relieving triangle. Today, this stands empty, but surviving fragments show that the façade was meant to dazzle. Flanking the huge bronze-sheathed doors, semi-engaged columns of dark green marble carved in geometric patterns rose from square-stepped bases. Their capitals were topped with further columns of red marble, between which, concealing the relieving triangle, stretched ornamental bands of rosettes and red marble spirals (like the marble for the columns shipped from quarries in the Mani, the centremost peninsula of the southern Peloponnese). Despite its having already been looted by the Roman age, it is little wonder that Classical visitors and tour guides thought that it had been a treasury associated with one of the richest Greek rulers of mythology. Conspicuously expensive in terms of scale, materials and resources – it is calculated that it must have taken 20,000 man days to construct – this was the

resting place of a ruler who was determined to demonstrate authority and wealth. It is a monument not to a city or a country but to an individual and his family, for there is evidence from other *tholos* tombs that they were used as mausoleums to house several generations of the dead.

Yet even now the Greek world was changing. Life was becoming harder; trade did not flow quite so freely; and protective walls were being reinforced – not least on the coast, some 20 km (12 miles) south of Mycenae, at the **Citadel of Tiryns**. When first built on its narrow rocky outcrop in the third millennium BC, Tiryns, one of Mycenae's several satellite cities, was only a few hundred metres from the sea, but by the thirteenth century, soil erosion and the build-up of sediment meant that the beach was almost a kilometre distant. Like Mycenae, Tiryns had been occupied for millennia – there are signs of habitation from as early as 5900 to 5400 BC – but it was

in around 2500 BC that it rose to greatness. The lower city bustled with lanes and houses, some perhaps the homes of merchants rich from the ships that tied up to the nearby quay; above, the citadel was topped by a massive circular structure, two-storeys high with a diameter of no less than 28 m (92 ft) and a façade supported and enhanced by jutting bastions. Towering on the highest point of the low hill, its upper walls constructed out of clay, its roof from terracotta tiles, it was a landmark for sailors tacking in across the bay and one unique for its age. Today its purpose is unknown – suggestions include a residence, a sanctuary, a fortress or (more prosaically) a granary – but what is certain is that, like the houses in the residential area, by 2200 BC it lay in ruins, destroyed by all-consuming fire.

A reconstruction of the thirteenth-century BC *megaron* of Tiryns' palace shows a throne on a raised dais to the left, as well as the round central hearth surrounded by four columns.

It took Tiryns a long time to recover. While the settlement was gradually restored, it would be five centuries before any kind of monumental building was erected on the citadel, and even then, it was unremarkable: a mansion straddling two shallow terraces linked by a workaday staircase. But in the middle of the fourteenth century, at around the time that neighbouring Mycenae became surrounded by its massive walls, Tiryns, too, was not only refurbished but strengthened. The mansion was knocked down, and its site levelled; a huge, sprawling palace was constructed, complete with *megaron* and antechambers, its walls plastered and painted. The upper citadel was ringed with walls, 10 m (33 ft) high, 6 m (20 ft) thick, Cyclopean and impregnable. In legend, this was home to Eurystheus, the jealous king, who delighted in obeying the goddess Hera's command to send his cousin Heracles to perform twelve increasingly dangerous labours, at first nearby (at Nemea and Lerna) but gradually more distant (Crimea, Spain, even the Underworld). Each time, flushed with success, Heracles returned to Tiryns, where later Greeks imagined its ruler cowering, terrified, in an amphora jar for his protection.

But Tiryns' people had more than an amphora to protect them and a braver king than Eurystheus. Around 1250 BC, when Mycenae's Lion Gate was being built, Tiryns received a new and even more impressive palace, with not one *megaron* but two, each frescoed and furnished with a throne and hearth, identical except for scale. Twice the size of the other, the larger *megaron* gave out onto the colonnaded great court, home to a round altar, the focal point of palace ritual. Now, too, more massive walls were built, this time 20 m (66 ft) high, complete with arrow slits, and embracing the entire lower citadel, with towers and well-protected staircases (two tunnelling deep into the rock to access cisterns), strong defensive gates (the main gate, like the Lion Gate at Mycenae, approached by a long ramp), and an impressive set of passageways with corbelled vaults. The east gallery had access to six vaulted chambers, each 3.4 m (11 ft) square; and the south gallery, 20 m (66 ft) long, 5 m (16 ½ ft) high and 1.5 m (5 ft) wide, five doorways leading into storerooms.

While the scale and ambition of these defences are formidable, they were eclipsed by an even more ambitious project: a dam some 10 m (33 ft) high and 300 m (990 ft) wide, 4 km (2 ½ miles) upstream from Tiryns, accompanied by the redirection of the water course responsible for bringing down much of the silt that caused the coastline to recede. It was a huge undertaking, and it may have been intended to allow the lower town to be expanded to the north, but while the engineering work was certainly completed, the project's second phase was not. However, although the determined fortification of Tiryns, Mycenae and other contemporary sites suggests preparation for attack and siege, warfare was not the cause of their decline. At the end of the thirteenth century BC a massive earthquake rocked the region, one of a series of tremors that was rippling through the eastern Mediterranean, accompanied by heavy rains, destroying settlements and disrupting trade routes. In time, these natural disasters would be accompanied by a breakdown in order, precipitated either by raiders from the sea or by civil unrest, as across Greece an old world disintegrated, and the age of kings came to an end.

The nature of the power relationship that had existed between these kings remains uncertain. Only a few centuries later, the first Greek epic poems, the *Iliad* and *Odyssey*, told of a network of palaces, each with its largely autonomous ruler, albeit subject to the overall leadership of Agamemnon, king of Mycenae. It was this fractious confederation that, according to mythology, was called upon to launch the thousand ships that sailed to reclaim the Spartan Helen when she eloped with Paris and so sparked the Trojan War. It was in turn the Trojan War that Greek, Roman and later scholars once blamed for the collapse of the Bronze Age. Taking Homer's poetry largely at face value, archaeologists looked for the sites of long-lost palaces, and while the premise on which they dug was misguided, it is thanks to their excavations that we now have a much clearer picture of the reality of Bronze Age life. Indeed, discoveries at two great monuments have rewritten Greek history. The first is at Troy itself.

Troy, too, was founded upon maritime trade. Strategically sited near the western mouth of the Hellespont – the channel, 61 km (38 miles) long and narrowing from 6 to a mere 1.2 km (from 3 ¾ miles to ¾ mile) wide, separating Asia from Europe – Troy sat on a low hill by a shallow sheltered bay, an entrepot for traders, a useful anchorage for merchant ships. For the waters of the Hellespont were as treacherous in antiquity as they remain today, when strong-gusting winds can turn currents racing down from the Black Sea to the Aegean at a speed of some three knots dangerously unpredictable and choppy. Even in calm weather it was impossible to navigate them under sail. Instead, they needed many hours of back-breaking rowing, so it was little wonder that those few Bronze Age captains who braved the voyage chose to weather storms and conserve energies in Troy's safe haven, or that the city formed a useful hub for trading goods brought overland.

Opposite: An Athenian black-figure vase (Antiope Group c. 520 BC) shows Achilles dragging the body of Hector around the walls of Troy, as the ghost of Patroclus hovers above his tomb.

Above: Regular vertical offsets and a slight inward inclination lend a sense of elegance and rhythm to the limestone walls of Troy.

Occupied from at least the early third millennium, by 2500 BC Troy was already an impressive settlement with more in common with later mainland Greek fortress cities like Mycenae than with the island palaces of Crete or Thera. A palisade enclosed 9 hectares (22 acres) of the lower town; high stone walls ringed the citadel; tall monumental gateways controlled access; and vast buildings 40 m (130 ft) long rose on the hilltop, great halls for public gatherings or worship. This was a time of immense wealth and conspicuous consumption, when rich Trojan women adorned themselves with precious jewelry – gold diadems and necklaces and earrings, their pendants delicate and fragile – and mansions boasted artefacts of gold and silver, lapis lazuli, carnelian, electrum, imported from the heartlands of Asia Minor and beyond. Around 2300 BC, this Troy was destroyed by sudden fire, but five hundred years later, as its lower town (surrounded by a palisade and ditches, and supplied with fresh water delivered through a system of artificial shafts and tunnels) trebled in size to 30 hectares (74 acres), its citadel (today known as Troy VI) once more rose proudly from the ashes.

It was now that the most striking iteration of the **Walls of Troy** was built. Constructed from shining limestone, some 10 m (33 ft) high and 5 m (16 ½ ft) thick, they slanted gradually inwards. Horizontally they seemed to ripple, thanks to a series of

regular vertical offsets: in other words, instead of curving, every 5 to 7 m (approximately 16 to 23 ft), the straight wall formed a slight acute angle, with each subtle corner protruding between 15 and 18 cm (6 and 7 ⅛ in.). These walls were fitted with impressive towers and gates, including one which, like the Lion Gate at Mycenae, was furnished with a bastion on its right side for maximal defensive capabilities. On the citadel itself, a well-paved street and lanes served a vibrant community of two-storeyed flat-roofed houses, bestriding the hill on terraces. From here, rich Trojans could gaze inland towards estates and farmlands rich with herds of cattle, sheep and horses, or out to sea where ships with linen sails and flaxen rigging brought crates of goods from the Aegean coasts, while in their pillared halls their wives and female servants stood at the loom, working garments like the double-folded purple cape adorned with images of flowers that Homer imagined Andromache weaving for her husband, Hector.

Evidence suggests that Bronze Age Troy was indeed dragged into hostilities – but not with Greece. Instead, it may even have

## 'IF AN ENEMY COMES FOR YOU ... I IN MY MAJESTY WILL NOT BETRAY YOU, ALAKSANDU.'

HITTITE CUNEIFORM TABLET, *c.* 1300 BC

Opposite: A Hittite clay cuneiform tablet from around 1280 BC outlines a treaty between the Hittite King Muwattalli II and Alaksandu of Wilusa, whose name transliterates into Greek as Alexander of Ilion.

Above: A watercolour reconstruction shows the citadel and town of Troy beside the great bay that it once dominated.

allied with Greeks against the mighty Hittite Empire and its capital at Hattusa, a sprawling city (whose gates, like Mycenae's, were guarded by stone lions) of 80 hectares (198 acres) in the heart of Asia Minor. Hittite documents tell of a war waged around 1400 BC against a coalition of cities from western Anatolia, which include Wilusa – identified as Ilion, an alternative Greek name for Troy. One document, a letter written subsequently by a Hittite king, implies that among those fighting in the coalition were soldiers of the Ahhiyawa, perhaps a form of the word 'Achaeans', a term that Homer uses for the Greeks. The letter, however, shows an interesting ambivalence towards these Ahhiyawa. Although, acknowledging their control of Millawanda (the city that Greeks called Miletus), its author changed his mind regarding how he wanted to address the Ahhiyawan king: a section that describes him as a brother (and therefore an equal) has been scored out. Another thirteenth-century BC letter speaks of an attack upon Wilusa by the Arzawans of Anatolia, which led King Alaksandu of Wilusa to enter an alliance with the Hittites – a further tantalizing detail, since Alaksandu sounds very like Alexander, another name by which the Greeks knew Troy's prince Paris, suggesting a further, if oblique, connection between myth and history.

Of the ten-year Trojan War (which Eratosthenes, the third-century BC philosopher and mathematician, calculated to have ended in 1184), there is no evidence. Around 1300 BC, Troy VI was indeed destroyed, but more likely by earthquake than by existential war, for it was soon rebuilt, its citadel more crowded than before, its lower city larger. But its salad days were over. A century later, fire swept through this city, too, and although it was again repaired, the workmanship was shoddier, the buildings less impressive. Artefacts used in its houses suggest that, while its population remained intact, increasing numbers of immigrants were moving in. Meanwhile for millennia, the local river Karamenderes (possibly Homer's Scamander) had been depositing its mud in Troy's once-sheltering bay, and it became so badly silted that it was barely useable. Today Troy stands 6 km (3 ¾ miles) inland. So, while the story of the Trojan War was so ingrained in the later Greek psyche, archaeology shows that it is little but a myth, perhaps based on woolly memories of war against the Hittites in which Troy and a Greek king were actually allies. Even the social fabric described in Homer's epic

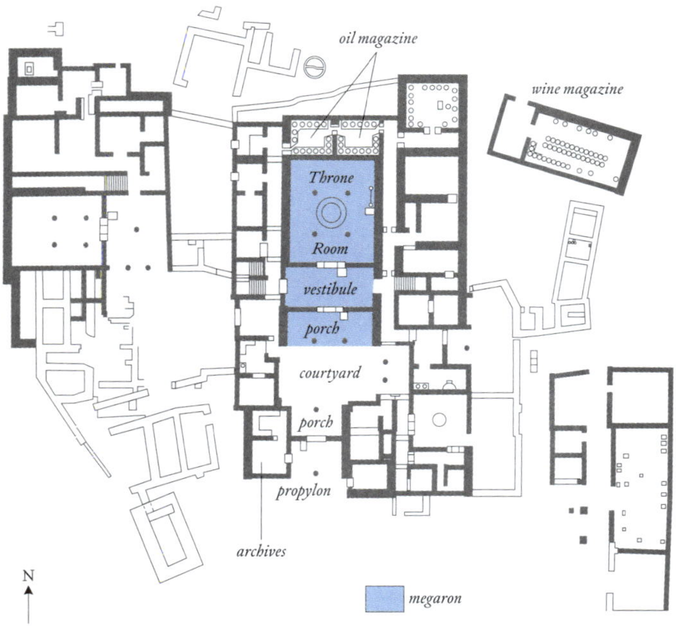

Opposite: A plan shows the layout of the Palace at Pylos. In Homer's *Odyssey*, Odysseus' son Telemachus spends the night sleeping in the portico near the records office.

Above: Dating from 1180 BC, this Linear B tablet from Pylos records a dispute between a priestess, Eritha (acting on behalf of her sanctuary), and the local community over a piece of land.

poems, so convincing to modern readers, appears to have been largely fictitious, as evidence from our final Bronze Age monument suggests.

It comes from the south-west coast of the Peloponnese, in the **Palace at Pylos**, which housed a remarkable, if largely nondescript, office complex close to the *megaron*. Like Mycenae, Pylos was situated inland, but unlike that citadel, Tiryns and Troy it was not surrounded by huge walls. Instead, it nestled in the fertile plain of Messenia, close to what is now called Navarino Bay, a wide gulf whose entrance is all but closed off by the long ridge of the island of Sphacteria and, on a long spit to its west facing the sea, the smaller, sandy, horseshoe bay of Voidhokilia. It was here that Homer imagined a great sacrifice being held, presided over by the regional king, Nestor. In both the *Iliad* and *Odyssey*, he is a well-respected, if somewhat garrulous, character, an elder who likes to offer sage advice and reminisce about his own experiences in earlier conflicts, and to judge by his palace Pylos' king was a typical Bronze Age ruler.

Occupied since at least 1800 BC, Pylos had close contacts with Crete. Ceramics were imported from the island, and mason's marks on stones built into a *tholos* tomb some miles north of Pylos are identical to others found at Knossos. It was clearly a thriving community. From 1600 BC onwards, the palace was almost constantly being enlarged or otherwise improved to

Left: Discovered in Pylos' so-called Griffin Warrior Tomb in 2015, this agate seal ring, dating from between 1630 and 1440 BC, shows two warriors fighting over the fallen body of a third.

Opposite: This reconstruction of the Palace at Pylos gives a good idea of its lush setting on a hilltop overlooking the fertile Messenian plain.

incorporate monumental buildings with ashlar façades; a Minoan-style courtyard; wooden columns set on stone-cut bases; plaster floors and painted walls; a *megaron* complete with upper gallery, its hearth 4 m (13 ft) in diameter; a bathroom; corridors; and nearby workshops dedicated to the making of perfume, using olive oil from the vast groves of Messenia. But it was just off the propylon, or antechamber to the *megaron*, that the palace's 'engine room' was found: two small offices, their walls originally lined with shelves, repository for the temporary records of the palace's large, efficient army of civil servants.

The discovery in the rubble of these rooms of a hoard of clay tablets revolutionized our understanding of the Greek Bronze Age. All were inscribed with writing in a style today called Linear B (to distinguish it from the earlier, largely Cretan, Linear A), and when deciphered, they were found to contain not epic poetry or accounts of battles, as many people hoped, but detailed documents pertaining to the running of not just the palace but the roughly 2,000 sq. km (772 sq. miles) of wider Pylos. They revealed a king (or *wanax*), who, far from being simply a carefree fighter, presided over the governors or vice governors of a total of sixteen or seventeen districts within two provinces, each with their own officials and workforce. They spoke not just of religious ceremonies but of tax collectors and inspectors who toured farms and villages, making exhaustive inventories. They recorded everything from details about people and their taxable income ('Eritha the priestess holds the lease of a communal plot from the village: 48 measures of wheat'), to luxury goods ('one ebony chair with golden back decorated with birds, and a footstool inlaid with ivory pomegranates'), vehicles, including chariots, carts, and sundry parts thereof ('six pairs of heavily-built wheels, unfit for service'). And they included the numbers of beasts in the fields.

But while it came as a shock to many that, instead of being a world of strutting heroes, society in Bronze Age Greece was subject to byzantine micromanagement, disappointment was tempered by the realization that the language in which the tablets were inscribed was clearly an early form of Greek. Even many of the gods they mentioned were familiar: Zeus; Poseidon; Hera; Ares; Dionysus. Clearly there was a straight continuum of language and religion, if not of social order, between the second and the first millennium BC. And why this mattered was that in Greece and across the eastern Mediterranean, in just a few short decades, the world of the Bronze Age was swept away. Indeed, it was the flames that burned the palace of Pylos around 1180 BC that preserved the Linear B tablets and the information they contained – the clay had not been intentionally fired. They were meant simply to be temporary, to be erased, discarded, when the

This watercolour reconstruction of a wall painting from Pylos shows a musician strumming his lyre while his song soars in the form of a bird.

information that they stored was transferred to another form of record written (ironically) on more perishable material; so they provide a snapshot of one year, albeit a year of great significance, which saw the sunset of a civilization.

The tablets suggest that Pylos was mobilizing its defences. Attacks were being expected from the sea, but the identity of these attackers is obscure. They torched the palace, but they could not erase its history, and in its ruins archaeologists have found artworks whose significance is just as telling as that of the Linear B tablets. Among them is a tiny agate seal, a mere 3.4 cm (1 ⅜ in.) long, discovered in the tomb near the palace. Dating to around 1450 BC, it contained not only the remains of a long-haired man, some 1.5 m (5 ft) tall, but also jewelry and combs, carved ivories, goblets of gold and silver, bronze weapons – and the sealstone. Perhaps made in Crete, it shows two warriors fighting over the corpse of a third, a scene that appears in Homeric epic. But the ring was made over 250 years *before* the traditional date of the Trojan War and more than 700 years before Homer's poetry was first written down. Like the Greek language, the image (its composition oft repeated on Classical vase paintings) was part of a longer continuum.

**'THE MUSE LOVED THE SINGER MOST OF ALL, BUT GAVE HIM GOOD THINGS MIXED WITH BAD, ROBBING HIM OF SIGHT BUT GIVING HIM THE GIFT OF HONEYED SONG.'**

HOMER
*Odyssey*

So, too, were the Homeric epics themselves. Set against a red background, a fragment of wall painting from the *megaron* at Pylos shows a long-haired musician dressed in robes with patterned horizontal stripes, sitting on a multicoloured rock and strumming a five-stringed lyre, while a large white bird soars, open-winged, away from him. He is almost certainly a bard, perhaps a singer of epic songs, precursors of the *Iliad* and *Odyssey*; a forerunner of Homer or Homer's fictional bard Demodocus, who entertains the mythical Phaeacians and their guest, Odysseus, on the island of Scherie. What is more, the bird is a metaphor, a visual representation of a poetic formula that recurs in Homeric epic, where speech that is listened to, that strikes home, is described as 'winged words'. The bird in the Pylian fresco *is* the song of the lyre-player, words and music captured, monumentalized in art.

The end of the Bronze Age came rapidly. All the great civilizations, including Egypt, Assyria and Babylon, collapsed, and by 1050 BC every Mycenaean palace and its associated town lay empty or in ruins. The cause of this catastrophe seems to have been a series of disastrous events, each on its own survivable, but which, combined, resulted in a perfect storm of earthquakes and pandemics, crop failure and drought, the consequence of a change in climate which would last for nigh on three centuries. For many mainland Greeks these problems may have been compounded by economies that were dangerously overstretched – the building projects in Mycenae, for example, probably came close to bankrupting the palace – and overly reliant on foreign imports. When merchant ships no longer plied the trade routes, they discovered that they could no longer function successfully. Dwindling resources led to civil unrest and migration in search of better lives. Pottery finds suggest that many Mycenaeans travelled east to the south-west Levant, where they became known as Philistines, their heroic, if ultimately empty, swagger encapsulated in the towering figure of the biblical Goliath.

While other societies, such as those of Cyprus and the Levant, recovered relatively quickly, Greece did not fully re-emerge from the collapse until the early eighth century BC. But life went on, and when society was strong enough that it could once again define itself in monuments, romantic memories of the Bronze Age played a major part in shaping its identity.

# II.

# THE ARCHAIC AGE

# BECOMING GREEKS

(*c.* 1050–490 BC)

BY THE LATE EIGHTH CENTURY BC the Greek world was not just recovering from its Bronze Age collapse but thriving.

With the climate stabilizing, harvests improving and populations growing, communities began to coalesce in city-states or *poleis*. These were areas of land, some relatively large, some tiny, each governed by a wealthy family or groups of families often backed by councils of their social equals, sometimes supported by popular assemblies, and generally administrated from an urban capital. But always the sea beckoned. Fired by a desire for trade, adventure or more fertile farmlands, young men swarmed into black ships and set course for foreign coastlines, where they intimidated or won over the existing populations and founded *poleis* of their own, albeit recognizing their old home as their *metropolis* (or 'mother city'). Before each expedition put to sea, it sought the blessing of Apollo's oracle at Delphi – just one sign (but an important one) of Delphi's growing influence and status – and soon Greek cities dotted shores from Sicily and Italy, south to North Africa and east to coasts of the Black Sea and Asia Minor. In time there would be well over a thousand.

Almost everywhere they went, these restless questing travellers adapted new ideas and concepts. The most significant was the alphabet formed exclusively of consonants used by the Phoenicians, ambitious venturers, whose dominance was spreading along Africa's north coast. By the mid-eighth century BC, Greeks had repurposed it for their own language, adding vowels to banish any risk of ambiguity and arguably democratizing literacy. Whereas in Bronze Age Greece, writing (Linear A and B) was used purely for administrative purposes, within decades of the new alphabet being introduced, two

Right: On this *krater* from around 735 BC, a man boarding a ship clutches the left wrist of a garland-bearing woman in a gesture associated with marriage.

Below: On the shoulder of the 'Dipylos Wine Jug' (750–735 BC) is one of the earliest vase inscriptions. Only the beginning is legible: 'Whoever of all the dancers dances with most grace ...'

towering works of literature were written down – the *Iliad* and *Odyssey*, epic poems ascribed to Homer – whose action centred on the Trojan War. Around the same time, Hesiod, a mainland poet, wrote two shorter epics: *Theogony*, on religion and mythology, and *Works and Days*, using agriculture to address the big questions of life.

Arguably both poets were mourning (or perhaps celebrating) a lost past. Hesiod called his own period an 'Age of Iron', of 'days endured in toil and misery', of 'death that strikes by night', while the men who once sailed across 'the yawning chasm of the sea in ships to Troy because of Helen of the shining hair' belonged to a 'more righteous, braver, godlike race of heroes, whom we call "demigods"'. But Troy was more than simply a stirring legend; Homer's epics played a vital role in giving Greeks a shared identity in their diaspora.

In the late eighth century BC (when the *Iliad* was being written and western Turkey was being colonized by Greeks), beside the ruined city, **CULT AREAS AT TROY** grew heavy with the smoke of sacrifices offered to the heroes of the Trojan War. One structure, built into the Bronze Age city wall a hundred years before and containing both an altar and a statue, was enlarged along with its associated sanctuary. A timber building was constructed, too, and – most impactful of all – a tall stone platform was erected, abutting the already ancient walls, that exploited the theatricality of its setting to the full. Studded with no fewer than twenty-eight paved circles, each roughly 1.8 m

(6 ft) in diameter, it was here, so archaeology suggests, that, after sacrifices and raised high above the plain of Troy, fires were lit and, in their flickering shadows, men feasted as they watched the sun sink low, telling stories of the Trojan War and honouring its heroes. A few years later, around 700 BC, a little to the north-west of the citadel, at a site called today 'The Place of Burning', a large oval hall was built to house around fifty Bronze Age cremation urns, the focus of further rituals involving feasting.

The location of these structures, monuments to the heroic dead, was fraught with significance. While the doors of Greek temples, homes to the immortal gods, opened east to catch the sunrise, shrines of heroes tended to face west, the setting sun a metaphor for physical mortality (even if heroes' spirits were believed to survive death). Nor was it just at Troy that sacrifices were being made to legendary heroes. In the late seventh century BC, on mainland Greece at Therapne, a mile or so south of Sparta on a hilltop high above the plain of the Eurotas river, a shrine with an associated altar was consecrated for the worship of the legendary Menelaus and his wife, Helen, whose abduction sparked the Trojan War.

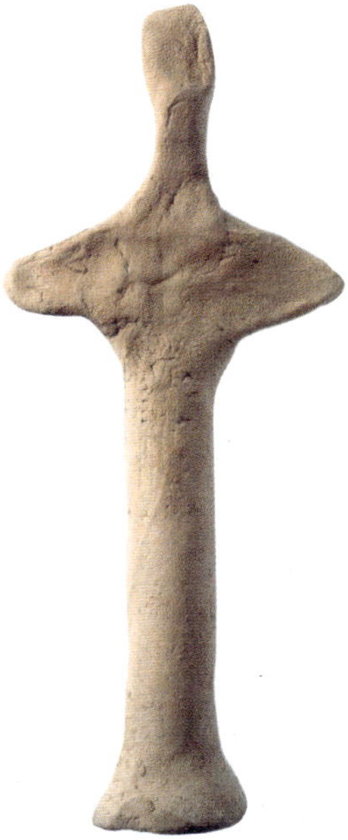

Opposite, above: The eighth-century BC cult area at Troy included altars and a stone platform for banqueting.

Opposite below: This terracotta figurine of a woman wearing a long dress and cylindrical headgear was discovered beside the altar in Troy's cult area.

Right: A terracotta amphora from around 540 BC shows Menelaus reunited with his wife, Helen, at the end of the Trojan War.

Known today as the **Menelaion**, it, too, was associated with ruins of a Bronze Age palace abandoned centuries before but visible in the Archaic Age. Positioned to maximize the impact of the sun setting behind the jagged ridges of Taygetus, the mountain range that towers across the valley, a ramp led up onto a platform supported by stone blocks 1.8 m (6 ft) high. Here sat a simple chapel with a footprint of approximately 5.5 × 8.5 m (18 × 28 ft), a tiled terracotta roof, cornices and pediments topped by disc acroteria (decorations at the apex of each pediment). In the second quarter of the sixth century BC the platform walls were reinforced and decorative triglyphs of blue limestone and white marble fitted. The chapel itself housed statues of Helen and Menelaus, here worshipped more as gods than heroes with choral song and dancing, and archaeology suggests that, like the Trojan hero-shrines, it was the focus of communal dining and the dedication of ritual offerings.

Many of these offerings survive – lead figurines of marching warriors with round shields and horsehair-crested helmets

gifted by the men of Sparta to the warlike Menelaus; bronze perfume flasks and statuettes of animals and ploughshares and elegant winged goddesses brought to Helen in her guise as both the loveliest of women and a powerful agent of fertility. A story in Herodotus' *Histories* illustrates the Menelaion's lure: a girl was born to one of Sparta's kings, so ugly that both parents despaired; so they instructed a servant to take her to the Menelaion every day, make offerings and pray for some improvement. One morning, the servant met a mysterious stranger, who insisted on holding the baby; after which the girl grew into the most beautiful woman in all Greece. She had, the Spartans were convinced, been cradled in the arms of Helen.

The shrines at Troy and Sparta spoke to Greeks' growing awareness of their past. But already on the island of Euboea a different type of hero-shrine had introduced a new design, the prototype of later colonnaded temples. The towns and villages of east central Greece and neighbouring Euboea were relatively unaffected by the Bronze Age collapse. Here, life continued much as normal, as evidenced by a settlement called today

Opposite: The so-called Menelaion at Therapne near Sparta is sited on a ridge above the Eurotas valley looking west towards the Taygetus mountains.

Right: British archaeologists excavating the Menelaion in the early twentieth century found numerous lead votive figures including mythological creatures and helmeted warriors.

Lefkandi, sited on a promontory on the west Euboean coast just south of the Euripus Strait that separates the island from the mainland. Archaeology reveals a thriving community, whose rulers, apparently enjoying the kind of lifestyle imagined in the Homeric poems, were buried with bronze vases, lotus-handled jugs and rings whose bezels bore the image of a ram-headed Egyptian god.

But it has also revealed a curious anomaly. In the eleventh century BC, a mere two or three generations after the collapse, a leading citizen – almost certainly Lefkandi's *wanax* (king or lord) – was cremated on a pyre of epic proportions. His ashes were wrapped in linen cloth, placed in a Cypriot bronze amphora (its rim decorated with scenes of animals and huntsmen) and buried in a shaft some 2.75 m (9 ft) deep alongside some of his possessions: an iron sword; a spear; a whetstone to keep his blades sharp for eternity; and four horses, their bits still in their mouths, his ritually slaughtered chariot team. There were further human remains – this time an inhumation – the skeleton of a woman, her feet crossed, her hands clasped over her belly, her hair originally twined with gilded coils, her neck adorned with not just necklaces of gold and faience beads but an antique Babylonian neckband, already a thousand years old, her breasts covered with gold discs embossed with spirals, and beside her head an ivory-handled iron knife. We cannot know what her relationship was either to the knife or to the man or whether she died naturally or endured the same fate as his horses, condemned to join the 'hero' on his journey into death. But if her burial is enigmatic, more enigmatic still is the monument erected over the remains.

Built of mudbrick on a stone socle (or lower course), its inner walls smoothed with plaster, the **Lefkandi Heroön** (or hero-shrine) was vast. At least 10 m (33 ft) wide and 45 m (148 ft) long, with a porched entrance (unusually) to the east and an apse at its west side, its interior was divided into three rooms of unequal size: a large hall with a central row of columns (apparently the scene of feasting) beneath whose clay floor lay the burials; and two smaller chambers near the apse. But it

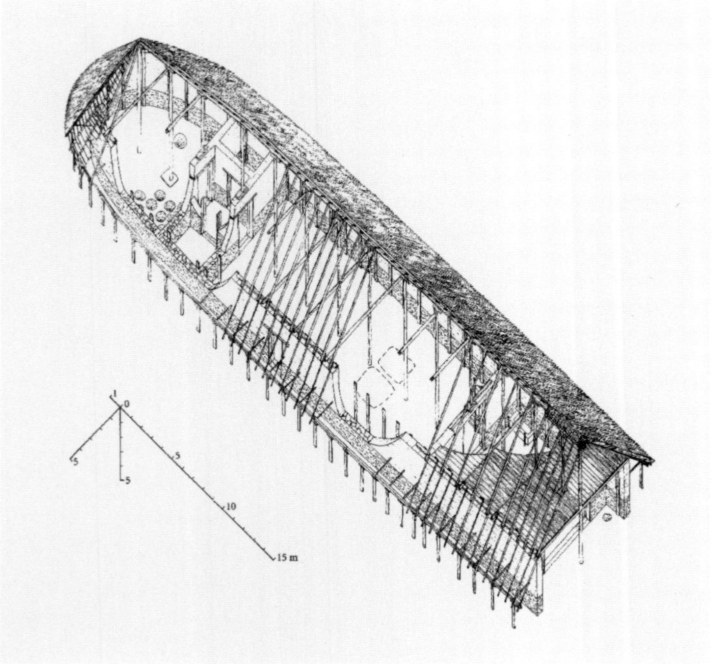


Below: This cutaway reconstruction of the Lefkandi Heroön reveals its sophisticated structure and layout.

Opposite, above: Dating from the early tenth century BC, this crescent-shaped gold sheet is decorated on its outer zone with triple spirals and on the inner zone with leaves.

Opposite, below: Discovered near the Lefkandi Heroön, this tenth-century clay figure appears to be an early depiction of a centaur.

was the exterior that was especially revolutionary. Regular post-holes show that the building was peripteral, in other words that it was colonnaded on each of its four sides, with rectangular wooden pillars supporting the overhanging reed-twined roof. Today the design is familiar from later stone and marble temples, but it is the first time that it was used for a Greek monument. The Lefkandi Heroön remains an outlier. For reasons that remain unknown, soon after it was built – and certainly by 950 BC – it was partially demolished and a mound thrown up above it, so, while its memory may have lingered on, it cannot have inspired later architects. As for Lefkandi, it continued to thrive, its people burying their dead with ever more extravagant grave gifts, until around 700 BC it was itself abandoned, relocated perhaps to nearby Eretria.

By now Euboea's influence was expanding. Its islanders were among the first to send out colonists, but other *poleis* quickly followed, and it was in one colony that the notion of a fully colonnaded temple was rediscovered. Strategically placed on trade routes between Greece and west-Greek colonies, Corcyra (modern Corfu Town) was founded by Corinthians, but as it grew more confident, relations with its *metropolis* broke down. In the mid-seventh century BC, the two cities clashed, fighting the first recorded sea battle in Greek history, and by 580 BC Corcyreans' wealth and self-belief were such that they

Left: A detail from a pediment of Corcyra's Temple of Artemis shows the terrifying face of Medusa, whose glance turned mortals to stone.

Opposite: Also on the pediment, Zeus hurls his thunderbolt against a fallen figure, probably a giant.

Overleaf: A reconstruction of one of the façades of the Temple of Artemis suggests its visual impact, which was further enhanced when the sculptures and architectural details were painted.

commissioned the erection of the first stone Greek temple. Like every one of its successors, it was modelled on earlier timber structures, but its permanence and cost in terms of time and raw materials were designed provocatively to trump Corinth.

Raised on a two-stepped platform, the **Temple of Artemis at Corcyra** comprised a *sekos* (the main rectangular box-like structure) of roughly 9 × 34 m (31 × 113 ft), whose wooden ceiling, some 15 m (50 ft) high, was supported by two rows of ten internal columns – and a peripteral colonnade, which enlarged the overall footprint by 6.4 m (21 ft) on every side. A statue of the goddess gazed from the echcing *cella* (nave) out east through double doors towards a massive altar, almost 25 m (82 ft) long and 2.75 m (9 ft) wide, where in a symphony of slashing knives many dozen animals could be sacrificed at once. Equally impressive and imposing were the sculptures that adorned the temple. Most arresting were two sets of painted high reliefs, set (for the first time in Greek temple architecture) into the pediments, the triangular gables dominating the two shorter sides.

'THE GORGONS, THREE WINGED SISTERS WITH THEIR SERPENT HAIR ... I WARN YOU: GUARD AGAINST THEM.'

AESCHYLUS
*Prometheus Bound*

At the centre of both was Medusa, the terrifying gorgon, with bulbous eyes, a chilling grin and lolling tongue. Dressed in a short tunic with snakes erupting from her shoulders and coiling round her waist, she seemed to be half-running, half-collapsing. All Greeks who saw the sculpture would know that in mythology Medusa could turn anyone she looked at into stone – a fitting subject, then, for this, the first stone temple. But they would know, too, that *this* Medusa was near death, because beside her were the offspring born out of her dying blood: the human hero Chrysaor and the winged horse Pegasus, which, captured in Corinth, threw off its rider before flying to Mount Olympus. The message was not especially subtle (for Pegasus read Corcyra), and the proliferation of Medusa's heads – many more appeared on fired-clay plaques arranged around the outside of the temple – was a defiant apotropaic: Corinthians be gone.

Flanking each pedimental Medusa were sinuous crouching leopards, symbols of power and wealth, while in the narrow corners of the west pediment were scenes of warfare – on the left,

an old man seated on a throne, his throat skewered by a spear, a fallen warrior behind him; and on the right a young Zeus hurling his thunderbolt at a fleeing older enemy, most probably a giant. The meaning of these compositions is obscure. Perhaps they too were meant as metaphors for Corcyra's relationship with Corinth: just as the youthful Zeus was killing the old giant and (perhaps) slaying the enthroned old king, so the young colony rejected its *metropolis*.

They were not the temple's only sculptures. Running above the architrave (the band above the columns) was a series of carved, painted blocks known as triglyphs, because of their three vertical grooves intended to resemble the cut ends of timber roof beam, interspersed with metopes, self-contained mid-relief figurative sculptures – an arrangement today known as a Doric frieze. Some metopes on this Temple of Artemis showed scenes from the Trojan War, evidence not just of the ubiquity of this myth in Greek culture, but the aspirations of Corcyreans positioning themselves as heirs to epic heroes. Their temple was, indeed, heroic, and it set a trend for centuries to come. Soon afterwards, another Corinthian colony, Syracuse in Sicily, raised

Below: James Stuart and Nicholas Revett's *The Antiquities of Athens* contains an illustration of Corinth's Temple of Apollo, which shows that more was standing in 1762 than does today.

Opposite: A vase painting from 380–370 BC shows a colossal statue of Apollo holding a bow in his left hand seen through the open doors of a temple.

> **'GODS TREMBLE WHEN APOLLO PASSES THROUGH THE HALLS OF ZEUS.'**
>
> HOMERIC HYMN TO APOLLO

a peripteral stone temple of its own, this time to Apollo, the sun god worshipped on Acrocorinth, the mountain at whose foot Corinth lay, and in 540 BC, Corinth herself erected an innovative Temple of Apollo. The architectural 'arms race' had begun.

Temples were more than monuments. For Greeks, the statues that they housed embodied the divine – some people believed that their cult images could sweat or show emotion – and literature imagined gods leaving Olympus for a while to visit favourite temples, as if vacationing in second homes. But temples were not simply religious buildings, designed to attract divine approval. They could also be political, since by projecting wealth and power, they suggested a city's special relationship with its patron gods – which was why ambitious *poleis* now competed to construct the most impressive temples.

The **Temple of Apollo at Corinth**, with its peristyle of tapering monolithic columns hewn from local limestone, was an innovative masterpiece. Sited on a low hill in the centre of the agora, the city's commercial and administrative hub, at 54 × 22 m (177 × 71 ft), it was marginally larger than its Corcyrean rival. It was also more sophisticated. Like the earlier Lefkandi Heroön, it contained more than one room: not just the east-facing *cella* housing the god's cult statue but a separate smaller west-facing chamber, known as an *opisthodomos*, entered

Opposite: Acrocorinth, the citadel of Corinth, dominates the ruined colonnade of the city's Temple of Apollo.

Below: A Lydian gold coin from around 560 BC found in the foundations of the Temple of Artemis at Ephesus shows a lion attacking a bull. Coins such as these may have been stored in Corinth's contemporary Temple of Apollo.

by its own impressive doors. The functions of this *opisthodomos* remain unknown, but it may have served as a shrine to the local hero Sisyphus, whose cult, closely connected with Corinth's agora, explored the boundaries between life and death. Legend told how, in a bid to cheat death, Sisyphus ordered his own corpse to remain unburied in the agora. Arriving in the Underworld, his soul gained permission to return to earth to organize his funeral; but, once reunited with his body, Sisyphus refused to renounce life, until Zeus sent Hermes, escorter of souls, to punish him. Forced back beneath the earth, he was condemned to push a boulder up a slope towards the upper world, but the stone kept slipping back and rolling down again. Being part of Corinth's most secure building, another function of the *opisthodomos* was to serve as *polis* treasury, housing booty, bullion and religious artefacts – perhaps including coins, since its construction coincided with the introduction of money by the Lydians, whose King Croesus was expanding his empire to include Greek cities on Asia Minor's north-west coasts.

Corinth's Temple of Apollo was also more sophisticated in design than any of its predecessors. For the first time in Greek architecture, its stylobate showed upward curvature – in other words, the platform on which the temple stood swelled slightly from each corner up towards the centre. The purpose was not just practical (allowing rainwater to drain off), it was aesthetic, too. The architect may have learned from Egyptians, who had long known that a large flat surface seen from a distance seems to bow. Upward curvature compensates for this, causing the observer paradoxically to see a straight line. It was the first time that this refinement had been used in Greece, but subsequent architects used increasingly sophisticated calculations to counter optical illusions and enhance a building's impact.

Thanks to mathematics, architects and engineers were making remarkable advances. Nowhere was this more evident than on the east Aegean island of Samos. By the mid-sixth century BC, the population of its main town had grown so much that its wells could no longer supply sufficient water, especially in the event of siege. So, an engineer from mainland Megara was commissioned to construct a tunnel running north to south through nearby Mount Kastro as part of an aqueduct diverting water from a constantly flowing spring. The **Tunnel of Eupalinus** was a triumph of precision engineering. Its scale was impressive enough – 1036 m (3,399 ft) in length (with one additional channel 890 m [2,920 ft] long leading from the spring to the tunnel mouth and another 1,006 m [3,300 ft] from the exit to the city), and while the northern part of the main passage was narrower, the southern half averaged 1.8 m (6 ft) in width and height. But even more remarkably, either to save time, or to show off his virtuosity, Eupalinus instructed diggers to begin from each end simultaneously. Given that the project would take at least eight years to complete, this was potentially risky, but Eupalinus had prepared meticulously.

First, he surveyed the mountain, choosing for the tunnel mouths locations of precisely the same height above sea level, and establishing a straight line between the two. Work now began, the excavators constantly maintaining their direction by looking back through the tunnel to its opening. All went well, until after some 275 m (900 ft) those excavating from the north hit an unstable section of rock. Undeterred, Eupalinus resorted to geometry, bypassing the unsafe area on a course describing two sides of an isosceles triangle. But now the workers were quite literally in the dark. They could not see the tunnel mouth, and at least once calculations had to be revised. At last, with only 12 m (40 ft) separating the two teams, diggers heard the blows of picks resonating through the mountain. The two halves of the tunnel were close to meeting. Now Eupalinus instructed his men to angle their course inwards towards the sound, at the same time increasing the height of the tunnel roofs to minimize the danger of their missing one another on the horizontal plane. He need not have worried. His calculations and his workforce's rigour meant that the floor levels diverged by just the merest fraction of an inch.

For its degree of planning and assurance, Eupalinus' tunnel outstripped any other Archaic Greek project, and not simply in its initial calculations. The danger of rockfalls in the southern half meant that in three sections the roof needed to be raised, forming an inverted V reinforced with large stone slabs. Worse, work at the spring's source on an oval-shaped reservoir, its stone roof supported on fifteen pillars, caused disruption and lowered the water level, meaning that the tunnel floor was now too high. Eupalinus was therefore forced to revise his design by installing a separate channel on the tunnel's eastern side, 4 m (13 ft) beneath floor level at the north entrance dropping to 8.5 m (28 ft) at the south. This carried terracotta pipes, whose design, too, showed forethought: the top quarter of each of its five thousand sections could be removed so that the water course could be regularly cleaned.

Eupalinus' impressively engineered tunnel burrows through Mount Kastro to bring water to the city of Samos.

Left: Now in ruins, the Temple of Hera on Samos was one of the largest and most imposing temples in the Greek world.

Below: Perhaps made in Crete, this seventh-century BC ivory figurine, originally with inlaid eyes, was dedicated at the Temple of Hera.

Because of its strategic military purpose, the aqueduct was intended to be hidden, but another monument on Samos was unashamedly flamboyant: a temple of Hera, begun during the reign of Polycrates (*r.* 540s–522 BC), whose title, *tyrannos*, derived from the local Lydian word *turan* (king) and soon took on the modern meaning of 'tyrant'. With a footprint of 55 × 105 m (181 × 345 ft), it was reckoned by Herodotus to be the largest of his day. Dominating a sanctuary some 6.5 km (4 miles) south-west of the city, the temple's *sekos* boasted a double colonnade on its two long sides with a triple colonnade to the west and east, and a deep porch supported by two rows of five columns. In the arms race of architecture it was a major escalation, but it was not the only massive temple in the region. Despite Herodotus' calculations, it was not even the largest. Across the sea at Ephesus, the Temple of Artemis, bedecked with sculptures

Below: A plan of Delphi's sanctuary shows the Siphnian Treasury (bottom left) standing beside the Sacred Way which winds up to the Temple of Apollo.

Overleaf: An aerial photograph captures a gods'-eye view of Delphi's magnificence. The foundations of the Siphnian Treasury lie to the left of the picture before the bend in the Sacred Way.

showing processions of worshippers and scenes from Greek mythology, may have been a foot narrower, but at 115 m (377 ft) it was noticeably longer than its Samian rival. It, too, bristled with columns, soaring over 19 m (62 ft) tall, all paid for by King Croesus of Lydia, whose empire had subsumed the area, but who continued to maintain cordial relations with the Greeks. In fact, the walls of his own temple of Cybele (the Anatolian equivalent of Artemis) in his capital at Sardis were adorned with scenes from Greek mythology, and he was keen to cement good relations with Artemis' brother Apollo, especially at Delphi.

By the mid-sixth century BC, Delphi was emerging as a major panhellenic sanctuary. Its Sacred Way, leading up the slope of Mount Parnassus to Apollo's temple, was beginning to be lined by treasuries, temple-like buildings where *poleis* could store and flaunt valuable dedications to the god. The most flamboyant was the **Siphnian Treasury**, constructed around 525 BC. Despite its small size, the Cycladic island of Siphnos was rich thanks to its gold and silver mines. Its treasury

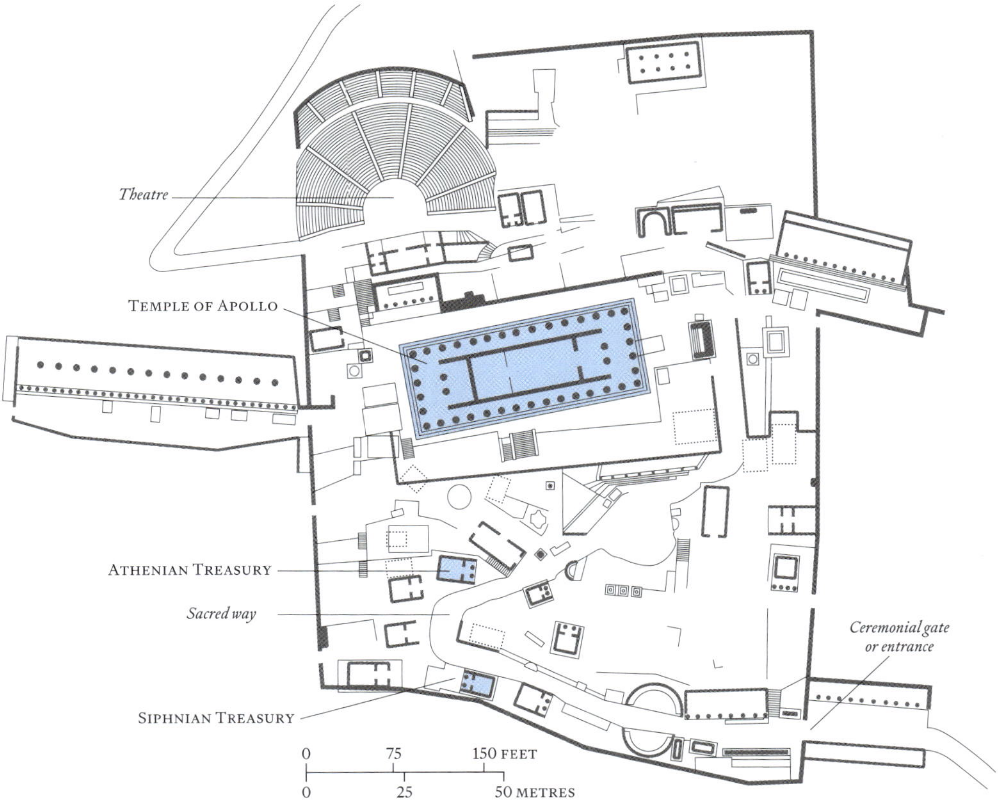

suggests that it was also ambitious, creative and unconventional. With a footprint of just some 8 × 6 m (27 feet × 20 ft), the building's basic structure was unremarkable: a *cella* and a porch, all topped by a gently sloping roof. But the materials employed all shouted wealth – marble shipped from Siphnos for the walls; marble shipped from Paros and Naxos for the frieze and pedimental sculptures.

Of the pediments only the eastern survives. Facing worshippers processing up the Sacred Way but actually at the treasury's rear, its sculptures showed an episode from Delphic mythology: Heracles trying to steal the sacred tripod, from which the oracle (a local woman chosen as Apollo's mouthpiece) regularly delivered prophecies. The composition brimmed with energy. Centre stage stood Zeus, intervening in the crisis, with Apollo to his left and Heracles to his right, both tugging at the tripod, and both flanked by other figures: Artemis, assisting her brother, Apollo; further deities or heroes; two chariot teams, one of whose horses reared violently; and in both narrow corners, looking on, reclining figures, one of the first times that sculptors solved how to fill this awkwardly diminishing space in such a way. Each figure showed sophisticated craftsmanship, while the decision to step back the flat façade behind them allowed torsos, arms and heads to be carved in the round, imbuing them with added vibrancy.

Above: A detail from the east pediment of the Siphnian Treasury shows Apollo and Heracles fighting for possession of Delphi's sacred tripod.

Opposite: The north frieze of the treasury showed the Gigantomachy, including this scene showing Apollo and Artemis fighting side by side and a lion savaging a giant.

Around the outside of the building ran an equally imaginative continuous (or Ionic) frieze. Surviving portions of the west frieze, once painted vividly like all the sculptures, with details such as wheels and reins affixed in metal, show Hermes (identifiable from his winged sandals and herald's wand) greeting the arrival of two four-horse chariots, each carrying a goddess. Since the right-hand section of the frieze is lost, it is impossible to tell what scene it shows, but it is probably the Judgment of Paris. If so, it suggested a prelude to conflict, and thus tied in with scenes sculpted on the building's other three façades.

The north frieze, flanking the Sacred Way, showed the Gigantomachy, the legendary conflict between Olympian gods and an older race of giants who tried to overthrow them. Increasingly popular in sixth-century BC Greek art, this battle was often presented as the divine equivalent of the Trojan War, another example of the triumph of Greek justice and order. It gave sculptors license to show off their skill, and nowhere more

Left: The chaos of war is brought to life on the sculptures of the Siphnian Treasury's north frieze. Here a goddess skewers a fallen giant, while a horse's hooves flail perilously near her head.

Opposite: A reconstruction of the west side of the treasury conveys its elegance and wealth of architectural detail.

so than here. The sheer brilliance of the work is astonishing, a melee of figures carved in high relief: helmeted warriors, some fighting in ranks, their round shields overlapping; Heracles coming to the aid of the Olympians; gods and goddesses, identifiable through iconography, striding through the fray, among them Apollo and Artemis firing volleys of deadly arrows; a chariot drawn by lions, one of which is bringing down a stricken giant: all organized with such precision that the composition is alive with impetus and drive without appearing messy.

The two remaining sides returned to the theme of the Trojan War. The south frieze, less visible and less well-worked, showed an abduction: magnificently rendered horses; an altar; a man lifting a woman onto his metal-wheeled chariot. This is most likely Paris and Helen leaving Sparta, the consequence of Paris' judgment shown on the east side, the cause of the war shown on the west, home to another remarkable composition. Here, observed closely by the seated gods, Greeks and Trojans in full armour are fighting over a fallen warrior, as the image of a gorgon's head leers from the central shield. Once more, deities and human heroes exist on the same plane, the fate of mortals central to the interests of the gods. Unusually, most figures on the Siphnian friezes are identified by name, the letters carved beside them. It was a technique familiar from vase painting, aiding the viewer, self-consciously underlining the scene's artifice, but somehow not interfering with its vibrancy.

What probably caught most visitors' attention, however, was not the frieze but the two over-life-sized sculptures of young women standing on raised platforms at the entrance to the porch, supporting the entablature in place of columns. While representations of the female form had been used as table legs or mirror handles, this was the first time that they appeared in architecture as what we now call caryatids. And these Siphnian caryatids were exquisite, their pleated dresses hanging in folds,

their well-combed hair cascading artfully across their shoulders, their earrings and jewelry fashioned from precious stones and metal. Stylized life-sized statues of young aristocratic women known as *korai* (maidens) were a common sight in sanctuaries such as the Athenian Acropolis, offerings made to gods and goddesses by grateful citizens. But, to date, this use of *korai* as columns was unique, and it would be copied only sparingly in centuries to come. Greek architecture was conservative; the Siphnian Treasury was not – and to religious-minded Greeks it may have seemed as if Apollo disapproved. Shortly after its completion, disaster struck the island: it was attacked by envious neighbours; coincidentally its mines flooded; and in the twinkling of an eye, it collapsed into obscurity.

While the Siphnian Treasury was being built, a short distance up the mountainside an even more ambitious enterprise was underway. In 548 BC an accidental fire had destroyed the sanctuary's most important structure, the **Temple of Apollo at Delphi**, and in the years that followed, its priests worked hard to raise sufficient capital for its replacement: a limestone temple whose more sizeable new footprint – 58 × 22 m (191 × 71 ft) – entailed considerably enlarging its foundations by constructing a huge polygonal wall. The costs involved were astronomical (equivalent to more than three and a half million days' pay for many citizens), but such was the cachet of the venture that it attracted substantial

Above: A partially coloured version of the Siphnian Treasury's west frieze showing Aeneas and Memnon with the body of Antilochus, all identified by name.

Opposite: An Athenian *krater* (450–400 BC) shows Apollo seated in his temple flanked by Doric columns and tripods. His bow and quiver suspended above him, he holds a laurel branch in his right hand.

Overleaf: Albert Tournaire's evocative reconstruction of Delphi, showing the Temple of Apollo towering over the treasuries, was made in 1900 when the site was being first excavated.

## 'KNOW YOURSELF; NOTHING IN EXCESS; PROMISES LEAD TO DISASTER'

DELPHIC MAXIMS

donations from Greek plutocrats and foreigners alike, including Egypt's pharaoh Ahmose II. However, after thirty-five years funds ran out.

Work stalled until the Alcmaeonids, a rich Athenian family in exile, offered not just to pay for its completion, but to build the east façade from expensive Parian marble (by now the go-to medium for any prestige project) – on condition that Delphi's priests persuaded Sparta to help restore them to their city. Within three years the temple was mostly finished, its *cella*, including a small chapel where the words of the oracle were spoken, paved with blue-grey marble slabs, its elongated *sekos*, ringed by columns (six on the shorter sides, fifteen on the long), its porch inscribed with maxims said to represent the wisdom of seven of the Greek world's greatest thinkers: Know Yourself; Nothing in Excess; Promises Lead to Disaster.

More visible, however, from the outside were the temple's pediments. At first sight, their subject matter was conventional enough. The west (limestone) pediment showed the Gigantomachy. While its sculptures no longer survive, a passage from Euripides' tragedy *Ion* reveals that it included Athena 'brandishing her gorgon-shield', 'Bacchus, loud-roaring, with his rod of ivy', and Zeus unleashing his blazing thunderbolt, a description which informs us about not just the pediment's appearance but how contemporaries viewed it – imputing sound and motion to static, albeit masterfully executed and vibrantly painted, sculptures.

As for the east pediment, its sculptures carved in the round from marble and set above the *cella*'s doors, it showed Apollo riding into Delphi for the first time on a four-horse chariot surrounded by a throng of mortal worshippers. Today, Apollo himself is lost, but fragments of other figures survive: torsos of three horses, their manes combed and dressed, one still equipped with its broken but proud head, and all emerging from the flat façade to tower above the viewer; shattered bodies of some worshippers, men nude as befitted heroes, women with well-tressed hair and patterned robes, standing four-square, gazing out across the temple's forecourt; and in each diminishing corner lions savaging their prey.

The sculptures exuded authority, but they also combined legend with living politics, pointing up Delphi's close relationship with its Athenian sponsors. The myth of the Gigantomachy was increasingly associated with Athens, but more specifically Apollo's arrival at Delphi and his temple there were linked to the exiled Alcmaeonid family. According to legend, Apollo reached Delphi from Delos (the island of his birth) via Athens, from where his hosts accompanied him across

Above: Even in ruins, Apollo's temple at Delphi is breathtaking, poised as if between heaven and earth in the folds of a high valley.

Opposite: In around 560 BC, the islanders of Naxos dedicated this monumental sculpture of a sphinx atop a column at Delphi as evidence of their wealth and prestige.

the same mountain road that the exiles took when they were expelled. Moreover, it was a member of those exiles' family who (with a friend, the *tyrannos* of Sicyon) had paid for the construction of the former Delphic Temple of Apollo, the one that had burned down. The pediment, then, provocatively set the Alcmaeonids centre stage beside Apollo himself, suggesting both their piety (expressed, too, by their largesse in funding the completion of the temple) and the validity of their demand to be restored to Athens. Small wonder that Delphi's priests kept their side of the bargain, or that the Spartans agreed to help the exiles return.

Apollo played a central role in Spartan life as he did in the lives of many Greeks, but in almost every other way Sparta was an anomaly. Formed of five separate settlements with no urban hub (and consequently no city walls), its territory was larger than that of any other *polis*, as in the late eighth century BC it expanded to control two regions, Laconia and Messenia (the entire southern Peloponnese), whose indigenous population it turned into helots (serfs). Now, dangerously outnumbered, Spartan citizens lived in constant fear of helot uprisings. So, to counter this home-grown threat, they entrusted all economic activities to a third class of residents, *perioikoi* ('surrounding residents'), and devoted themselves to harsh discipline and tough military training. Aged seven, boys were removed from mothers and brought up in barracks until, following a rigorously physical education, they were enlisted as citizens (known as *homoioi*, or 'identicals'), who for years continued to live and dine in communal messes, sharing food grown on the estates that each was allocated. All could attend political (or military) assemblies, voting not by a show of hands but by shouting on measures proposed by an annually rotating board of five ephors (overseers). These ephors held great power, dominating the *gerousia* (senate), and were even able to discipline the two kings, each from an old Spartan family, who reigned concurrently, commanded the army and presided at important state festivals.

Spartans were especially religious. Their calendar was studded with festivals, among them one in honour of Apollo held in a rural sanctuary at Amyclae. Here, legend told, he accidentally killed his lover Hyacinthus, buried the young man and caused flowers to blossom named in his honour and marked with the letters 'AI AI' (the sound Greeks made in lamentation), before revitalizing the boy and taking him to Mount Olympus. Every year in early summer, Spartans marked Hyacinthus' death and resurrection with a three-day festival which moved

emotionally from grief and solemn sacrifice to celebration, and physically in procession from the main cluster of Sparta's villages around its low acropolis to Amyclae, a few miles south. Here they staged athletic, hippic and music contests, held banquets and made offerings: grave gifts for Hyacinthus; a ritually woven tunic for Apollo.

God and hero were fused in a monument that dominated the sanctuary, the **THRONE OF APOLLO**. Designed by Bathycles of Magnesia in the early sixth century BC and subsequently extended, it was as flamboyant as the Siphnian Treasury but on an altogether vaster scale. At its heart was the hero-shrine, Hyacinthus' supposed tomb, with a bronze door through which offerings were passed, and, in front and to the right of it, an altar. So far so relatively conventional. But Amyclae was not just about Hyacinthus. It was about Apollo, too, and brilliantly Bathycles transformed the tomb to emphasize the close relationship between the god and hero, for rising above it, he set a colossal statue. This 14-m (45-ft) tall Apollo, its wooden frame plated in bronze, had (according to Pausanias, who damned it as 'unskilled'), 'a face and feet and hands, but the rest of it is more like a bronze pillar. It has a helmet on its head and carries a spear and bow'. Unskilled or not, glinting in the baking summer sun or glimmering in moonlight, it must have seemed alive with a divine energy – especially when seen within the context of its setting.

For the towering statue was framed on three sides by a huge throne-like construction containing several empty 'seats', each with a plinth beside it. Supported by statues of two Graces and two Seasons, and flanked by other figures from mythology, the Throne of Apollo teemed with painted sculptural reliefs. Pausanias refuses to describe them all lest he bore his readers. But it is apparent that, along with scenes of apotheosis (appropriate for Hyacinthus' own transformation), almost every myth from every part of the Greek world was represented – including the Judgment of Paris and other episodes from the Trojan War – a deliberate, some might say cynical, attempt by Spartans to appropriate a panhellenic heritage as they laid claim to be the rightful leaders of all Greeks.

Arguably, however, the true melting pot of Greek identity was sited 96 km (60 miles) north-west of Sparta at the rural sanctuary of Olympia. Nestling in a fertile valley at the confluence of two rivers 16 km (10 miles) from the sea, by the early eighth century BC, this sanctuary, the Altis, was home to a four-yearly festival in honour of Zeus of Mount Olympus (hence

Below: As late as the reign of the Roman emperor Gallienus (d. AD 268), the statue of Apollo at Amyclae appeared on coins minted in Sparta.

Opposite: There have been many attempts at reconstructing the Throne of Apollo. One of the earliest is this one, dating from 1815 and based on Pausanias' description.

its name, 'Olympia'), which included a footrace over a *stadion*, or 'stade' (*c.* 210 yards or 192 m). Greeks reckoned that the first festival was held in 776 BC, which they considered their 'Year One', using it as a terminus from which to date all subsequent events. Originally a local gathering, the Olympic festival was soon attracting participants from an increasingly wide area, at the same time introducing further athletic and hippic contests, so that by the early sixth century BC it was the foremost panhellenic gathering, attended by worshippers and contestants from across the Greek diaspora.

It was now (around 590 BC) that the **TEMPLE OF HERA AT OLYMPIA** was built within the Altis. At first sight two things seem curious: that this key sanctuary's first peripteral temple was dedicated not to Zeus but to his wife; and that it was not built out of marble. Instead, its tripartite *sekos* (porch, *cella* and *opisthodomos*) had walls of mudbrick on a limestone socle, pediments topped with immense stone disc acroteria 2.4 m (8 ft) in diameter, and a terracotta roof. It was also more elongated than most temples, with six columns on the short sides and sixteen on the long – a footprint of 51.5 × 19.2 m (169 × 63 feet). But most surprisingly of all, like the entablature, not just the peripteral colonnade but the interior columns, too (two longitudinal rows supporting the ceiling), were hewn from timber. Perhaps this reflects the relative poverty of Skillous, the tiny local *polis* that commissioned the temple; or perhaps it suggests a deliberate attempt to ensure that it blended with its rural setting – unusually the Altis was not part of any major settlement, and for much of the year the site was tranquil and unvisited. In time, however, with Olympia a magnet for rich dedications, the wooden columns were thought to be too rustic, and as each one cracked or rotted it was replaced in stone, each subtly different from the rest.

But why dedicate this first Olympic temple not to Zeus but to Hera? In fact, Pausanias saw two statues in the *cella* side by side – 'Hera seated on her throne with Zeus standing next to her, bearded, helmeted; both showing crude workmanship.' Originally both gods may have shared the temple. They certainly shared the sanctuary, and there were even two sets of Olympic Games: those sacred to Zeus, exclusively for men, from which women were barred on pain of death; and those sacred to Hera (held halfway through each four-year cycle) which were exclusively for women.

In the afterglow of the Archaic Age (according to Herodotus), a now anonymous Athenian defined what

Below: An early fifth-century BC Athenian red-figure vase shows an athlete preparing to throw the discus.

Opposite: A reconstruction published in 1896 shows the Temple of Hera at Olympia, its pediment capped by a distinctive stone disc *acroterion*.

constituted Greek identity as 'a kinship in blood and speech, the shrines of gods, the sacrifices that we have in common, and the likeness of our way of life'. He could have added the Greeks' love of competition, encapsulated in the *Iliad* as 'always to be best and to surpass all others'. Nowhere were these characteristics more apparent than in Zeus' festival at Olympia, which celebrated both shared identity and communal rivalry in not just sport but the extravagance of offerings made by *poleis* to win favour with the gods – and provoke human envy. The Altis shone with bronze and marble sculptures showing victorious athletes, chariot teams and legendary heroes, and in time a row of nine exquisite treasuries would stand on a low ridge above the

Opposite: An aerial photograph of the Temple of Hera from the east shows its tripartite floorplan.

Right: Pausanias' description of the antique ivory 'Chest of Cypselus' in Hera's temple formed the basis for this reconstruction published in 1815.

Below: Dating from around 590 BC, this stone head of Hera was part of a colossal statue dedicated in her temple at Olympia by the Spartans.

Overleaf: Replicas of the lions dedicated by islanders from Naxos still guard the terrace above Delos' sacred lake.

Temple of Hera while the temple itself housed such valuable objects as an antique ivory chest decorated with scenes from mythology, an ivory-faced couch believed to have belonged to the wife of one of the Games' founders, and an antique bronze discus inscribed with the wording of the truce sworn by every *polis* before each Olympic festival, guaranteeing a safe passage to participants.

Despite shared kinship, however, much divided the Greeks, not least ethnicity. Different ethnic groups could be identified thanks to specific customs and – more obviously – dialect. The two most significant were the Dorians (to which the Spartans belonged) and the Ionians. Tracing their lineage back to the legendary Athenian King Ion, these Ionians lived in scattered *poleis* in Sicily and south Italy but clustered more densely on the western Anatolian coast and the Aegean islands, one of which, Delos, they considered sacred to Apollo. Delos was the site of a quadrennial festival, where, according to the *Homeric Hymn to Apollo*, 'Ionians in long flowing robes assemble with their children and their modest wives ... To see them thronged there, you would think them ageless and immortal, gazing on their beauty, delighting in the men and the deep-bosomed women, in their sleek ships and in all their treasures.'

Naturally, Ionians used Delos, too, as a competitive venue, whether they were vying in the festival's athletic games or in the quality and cost of dedications to Apollo. Among the most impressive was the **Terrace of Lions**, a monument erected by

islanders of Naxos in the first half of the sixth century BC. At a time when many Ionian *poleis* such as Samos and Siphnos could boast prodigious wealth, the Naxians more than held their own, and their dedication proved them to be wealthy international sophisticates. Almost certainly modelled on avenues of sphinxes in Egyptian sanctuaries, the lions (originally at least twelve, though only nine survive) were positioned on a low rise that overlooked the sacred lake, next to which, beneath a palm tree, Apollo was believed to have been born. Carved in the round from marble quarried on Naxos itself and dominating the sacred Delian landscape, each lion, 1.6 m (5 ½ ft) tall, squatted on a rectangular plinth, its ribs clearly visible as it lifted itself up on its front paws, mouth open in a silent roar. Individually, each creature was magnificent. Collectively they exuded confidence and power. Part religious, part political, it was a robust if none-too-subtle metaphor: the Naxian ruling family as a pride of roaring lions asserting dominance over the prime sanctuary of the Ionians, and by extension the Ionians at large.

Given the vibrancy and creativity of Ionia, this was a controversial claim. For here in the Archaic Age the intellectual world was shifting on its axis, as early scientists and abstract thinkers probed the workings of the universe and questioned long-held beliefs. One, Anaximenes of Miletus, claimed that, far from being divine, stars were formed from fire, and heavenly bodies moved around the earth. Some doubted the very nature of the gods. Dismissing traditional religion, Xenophanes of Colophon wrote that 'if oxen, horses or lions had hands and the

Above: An imaginative reconstruction by Henri-Paul Nenot suggests the opulence greeting Classical visitors to Delos.

Opposite: A mid-seventh-century BC amphora found on Melos shows Apollo in a chariot drawn by winged horses being greeted by his sister, Artemis.

ability to use those hands to draw and fashion things as men can, horses would have drawn their gods like horses, oxen would have drawn their gods like oxen, and each creature would have made their gods identical to themselves.' Instead he posited 'one god ... in no way similar to mortal men in body or in thought'.

But such men were exceptions. For now, most Greeks still followed their traditional religion, repeating old tales from mythology, some telling of regime change and the death of kings. Occasionally fact mirrored fiction: in the mid-sixth century BC the leading Naxian family was ousted; a puppet prince was placed upon the throne; and dominance over Delos passed to a new, emerging superpower. It was all the work of a determined visionary strongman: Peisistratus, who in 546 BC installed himself as *tyrannos* of Athens.

Athens was already flexing her muscles. Twenty years earlier, in 566 BC, her ruling aristocrats had instituted a new four-yearly festival, the Greater Panathenaea, whose origins they said lay in Athena's victory celebrations following the Gigantomachy, a myth which the Athenians now co-opted as peculiarly their own. While the Greater Panathenaea never reached the heights of rival panhellenic gatherings at Olympia, Delphi, Corinth and Nemea, it helped establish Athens as an important player on the Greek stage, something that Peisistratus was keen to build on. So, he developed further festivals, such as the Eleusinian Mysteries, which promised a carefree afterlife and the City or Great Dionysia sacred to the god of transformation, Dionysus. At its core were competitions in the newly honed artform of tragedy. While other *poleis* had their own forms of drama and imitative performance, Athenian tragedy was unique, part religious ritual, part spectacle, part forum for discussing moral questions and part entertainment. The Great Dionysia took place in the city, where the audience sat on specially constructed wooden bleachers in its agora, but such was the popularity of drama that many towns and villages in Attica (the area surrounding Athens) soon built theatres of their own.

One of the most notable was the **THEATRE AT THORIKOS**, a town on Attica's east coast which owed its wealth to its association with local state-owned silver mines at Laurium. Although subsequently enlarged and enhanced, its basic form can still be seen. It was a shallow rectangle – in its final form, the flat *orchestra* (or dance floor), with an area of 16 × 27 m (52 × 89 ft), was wrapped on three sides by up to twenty-one banked rows of seats, stretching 55 m (180 ft) along the long north side. Remarkably, unlike the early theatre in Athens itself, even in their first iteration these seats appear to have been made of local limestone, a major commitment to the structure's permanence, but one perhaps explained by the ready availability of labour in the form of local mining slaves.

In later decades theatre design became increasingly sophisticated. During one performance in the early 490s BC, the timber scaffolding in Athens' temporary auditorium collapsed, causing the deaths of several spectators and prompting the theatre's relocation to the south side of the Acropolis, whose slopes were landscaped to accommodate tiers of wooden benches arranged in straight lines around three sides of a rectangular *orchestra*, while on the fourth a *skene* (or stage building) was erected to double as a backdrop to productions and a dressing room. Within decades, cranes were hoisting actors high above the *skene*'s roof to simulate flying gods, while wheeled platforms were being rolled out through its doors revealing scenes of horror carried out inside the 'palace'. As at Thorikos and other theatres spreading rapidly across the Greek-speaking world, Athens' Theatre of Dionysus was used for a range of purposes, not just drama but political gatherings, too, and already in these early days there was much to be discussed.

Peisistratus died peacefully in 527 BC, leaving two sons, Hipparchus and Hippias, to rule Athens and continue enhancing the city. This they did both architecturally (it was now that the Theatre at Thorikos was built) and culturally (attracting leading poets to Athens, including Polycrates of Samos' favourite, Alcaeus). But work on their most ambitious monument, a huge

**'HAIL TO YOU, DIONYSUS THICK WITH GRAPES! GRANT THAT THIS SEASON BRINGS US JOY!'**

HOMERIC HYMN TO DIONYSUS

Above: Close to the sea in eastern Attica, the Theatre at Thorikos is one of the earliest to survive.

Overleaf: From above, the design of Thorikos' theatre with its stone-hewn seating becomes immediately apparent.

limestone Temple of Olympian Zeus – which, on a platform measuring 41 × 108 m (135 × 354 ft) and surrounded by a double colonnade, was intended to rival the temples of Samos and Ephesus – was cut short when their regime was violently overthrown. In 514 BC, Hipparchus was assassinated as he prepared for the procession at the Greater Panathenaea, and two years later Hippias was expelled along with the rest of his family by Cleisthenes, the exiled rival backed by both Sparta and Delphi, whose new Temple of Apollo he had helped to fund, and who now returned home in triumph. After a brief period of turbulence, Cleisthenes restored stability by overhauling Athens' constitution and significantly increasing the authority of her approximately forty thousand citizens, making them eligible not just to vote on proposals put to their Assembly but, chosen randomly by lot, to hold many key offices of state. He called this constitution *isonomia* ('equality under the law') but it soon became known as *demokratia*, from *kratos* ('power') and *demos*, meaning both 'the people' and 'the poor'.

Democratic Athens was quick to monumentalize her radical new constitution, relocating the agora, the city's semi-sacred

public and commercial heart, to a space north of the Acropolis where Hippias' palace had once stood, and (preserving the unfinished Temple of Olympian Zeus as a monument to hubris) embarking on an ambitious building programme. This included demolishing and reconstructing the Temple of Athena Polias (Athena Who Protects the Polis), the city's spiritual heart, on the Acropolis, adding pedimental sculptures showing the goddess fighting in the Gigantomachy and building a row of administrative buildings in the agora, including on the site of Hippias' palace. Adorned with pediments and columns, metopes and triglyphs, some took their inspiration unashamedly from what was previously exclusively religious architecture. Another, the Royal Stoa, home to the office of a leading magistrate with legal and religious duties, was the first colonnaded hall (or stoa) to be built outside a sanctuary. The message of these monuments was clear: democracy was godlike and deserved to be venerated.

Meanwhile, that democracy found a new home. On the Pnyx (a hill overlooking the Acropolis and agora) houses were demolished and the ground landscaped into a vast half-bowl-shaped auditorium with a speaker's platform at its base. The seat of the Athenian Assembly, it could accommodate six thousand citizens, a fraction of the total population, but an improvement on the previous autocratic system. Throughout wider Attica, too, temples and sanctuaries were built or modified to celebrate the new democracy, but one monument stood out above all others.

The **Statue of the Tyrannicides** marked the first, and for a century the only, time that sculptures of contemporary or recently dead mortals were allowed to be erected in the agora. This was precisely the point, for it commemorated the two men, Harmodius and Aristogeiton, who killed Hipparchus back in 514 BC, and so (according to the disingenuous narrative favoured by one political faction) began the struggle for democracy. There are no records to suggest its appearance, but, sculpted in the last decade of the sixth century BC, it was considered so important that after it was looted two decades or so later, a replacement was installed, the work of Critius (the pupil of its original sculptor, Antenor) and Nesiotes. Of this we do have copies.

Cast in bronze and slightly larger than life-sized, it showed the two assassins striking their blow for freedom. His cloak draped over his left arm, a knife gripped in his right hand, Aristogeiton, bearded, older, advanced menacingly, while beside him Harmodius clutched an empty scabbard in his left hand as

**'GREAT WAS THE LIGHT THAT FLARED FOR THE ATHENIANS WHEN ARISTOGEITON AND HARMODIUS KILLED HIPPARCHUS.'**

SIMONIDES

An Attic *stamnos* (container for liquid) of around 470 BC is decorated with a scene showing the assassination of Hipparchus, the pose of the tyrannicides clearly based on the statue by Critius and Nesiotes.

he brandished his drawn sword above his head. Treated with wax to make the skin appear to glow, their eyes painted or inlaid with marble, the statues stood on their plinth beside the Panathenaic Way as it traversed the busy agora. They were not intended to be lifelike portraits of real people; instead, they were idealized representations of an inner heroism expressed through physical perfection. Their well-honed muscles and dispassionate expressions, like their heroic nudity, transcended reality to demonstrate the superhuman status the two men had achieved through action and self-sacrifice – since, like all heroes, they were dead, caught and killed in the immediate aftermath of the assassination. Despite not being connected to an altar or a shrine, despite the subjects' physical remains being buried in a nearby cemetery, despite the fact that many who now saw the sculpture had once known Harmodius and Aristogeiton when they lived, the statue of the tyrannicides did something very new in Greek monumental art: it elevated contemporary humans to the rank

of the heroic, halfway to the divine, and by the fourth century BC offerings were being made before the statue as if to heroes.

In its first iteration, the monument may have shown less motion and plasticity, perhaps resembling the towering *kouroi* (male equivalents of *korai* statues) which citizens of Argos set up at Delphi to commemorate the piety of two youths, Cleobis and Biton, who died after dragging their mother in a wagon in the

Opposite: The Statue of the Tyrannicides remained influential in the Roman period, as this marble copy of Aristogeiton from the second century AD attests.

Right: This Roman copy of Harmodius' statue was intended to stand beside the statue of Aristogeiton shown opposite.

heat to the sanctuary of Hera miles from their city. These *kouroi* demonstrate the rigid formalism of Archaic art inspired by statues seen in Egypt and the Near East and characterized by their forward-facing stance, their arms held stiffly by their sides, one foot advanced, an enigmatic smile about their lips. In the seventh and sixth centuries BC a craze for orientalizing sculptures had swept through the Greek world as it strengthened diplomatic and commercial ties with empires such as Croesus' Lydia and established trading posts in Egypt.

But in 550 BC events were set in motion whose impact was felt for centuries, when Persia's King Cyrus II annexed the

neighbouring Median Empire. Soon Babylon fell, too, and Egypt, and Lydia, and by 530 BC all Ionia was under Persian rule. Most Greek rulers accepted the new reality with grudging pragmatism: so long as they paid tax to Persia, they could maintain their lifestyle. But some were not so lucky. When Polycrates of Samos offended the local Persian governor, he was crucified, and by 499 BC many Ionians were so disgruntled that, inspired by Athens, they declared themselves democracies and rebelled from Persia. In early fighting, aided by Athenians, they burned much of Sardis – including (accidentally) Croesus' Temple of Cybele – but they were no match for an empire that

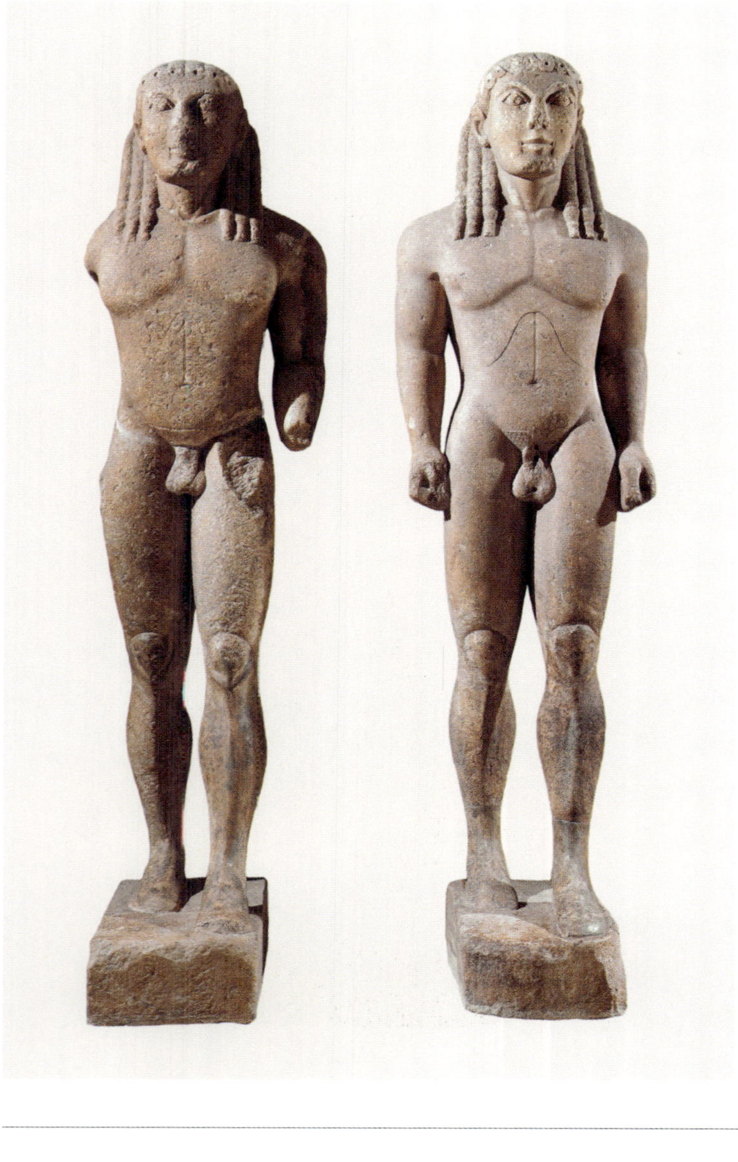

Left: We are familiar with the later Statue of the Tyrannicides, but the original late sixth-century BC version may have been more like the Archaic statues of Cleobis and Biton dedicated at Delphi by citizens from Argos.

Opposite: Dating from the third century BC, the so-called Elgin Throne is carved with the Statue of the Tyrannicides on one side (detail, above) and King Theseus killing an Amazon on the other (below), representing the Athenian democracy's victory over internal and foreign enemies.

stretched as far as India. By 493 BC the Ionian Revolt was crushed, and the vengeful Persians turned their sights on mainland Greece.

Three years later, their fleet was crossing the Aegean Sea, its mission: to destroy Athens and her democracy, to subjugate the Greeks and to install the exiled tyrant Hippias as Persian governor. The next months and years would see the most substantial shift in Greek affairs since the collapse of Bronze Age palace culture. As Naxos and Eretria burned, other *poleis* scrambled to respond to Persia's threat, some by capitulating, others by attempting to stay neutral, a few by mounting what seemed to be a doomed resistance. But one thing was clear: the relationship not only between east and west but between Greeks themselves had reached a tipping point. Society was changing. The Archaic Age was over.

# III.

# THE CLASSICAL AGE

# THE FIFTH CENTURY BC

(490–404 BC)

IN THE END, only Athens and the tiny *polis* of Plataea mobilized against the Persian army, so they thought it miraculous when, heavily outnumbered, they won a crushing victory at Marathon in 490 BC, forcing the enemy to call off the invasion. While the Persians lost 6,400 men, just 192 Athenians were killed, and their city commemorated them with an extraordinary monument, cremating their bodies and burying their ashes on the battlefield itself beneath a huge earth mound which was deliberately modelled on the gravemounds heaped above dead heroes in the epic tales of Troy.

Towering 12 m (40 ft) tall and with a diameter of 50 m (165 ft), this **SOROS**, as it is called, dominated what soon became in essence a rememberance park. Nearby, a smaller gravemound covered the remains of the eleven Plataeans who had lost their lives, while, at the spot where it was clear the battle pivoted in the Greeks' favour, they set up a 'trophy' (from the Greek 'to turn'). Usually, such trophies consisted of a suit of captured armour nailed onto a tree or hastily made cross, but here at Marathon the Athenians raised an Ionic column over 9 m (30 ft) in height and fashioned from local Pentelic marble, a proud, permanent memorial.

Nonetheless, the focus of this sacred landscape was always meant to be the Soros, the most conspicuous war grave of democratic Athens. The Athenians exploited its potential in every way they could. Around its base they set ten marble slabs – one for each of the ten 'tribes' or wards to which every citizen belonged, and which doubled up as regiments when on campaign – and on them they inscribed the name of each of the fallen. It is the first such war memorial in Western history.

**'AT MARATHON ATHENIANS FOUGHT IN THE FRONT LINE FOR GREECE, AND SCATTERED THE GOLD-GARNISHED PERSIANS' POWER.'**

SIMONIDES

Above: The Soros at Marathon. Following the battle in 490 BC, the Athenian dead were buried with full honours on the battlefield.

Overleaf: John Varley, *The Plains of Marathon*, 1834, showing the Soros with the Bay of Marathon and island of Euboea in the distance. Varley mistakenly inscribed his painting 'Tumulus of the Persions [*sic*] who fell at Marathon'.

But the message of the Soros was not just aimed at Athens. On an eleventh slab they carved two lines commissioned from their leading poet, Simonides: 'At Marathon Athenians fought in the front line for Greece, and scattered the gold-garnished Persians' power.'

Sidelining the Plataeans, emphasizing Persia's wealth and, by omission, reminding all who read it that Spartans had played no part in the victory (they had excused themselves, pleading the need to celebrate a festival), the couplet spotlit Athens' role as saviour of all Greece and thus her claim to be its leader.

The Athenians believed it was a message worth repeating. On their acropolis, they raised a statue, in response to an apparent promise to Athena by Callimachus, their commander-in-chief, who was killed at Marathon. It was an Ionic column, almost 4 m (13 ft) high, topped by a 4.5-m (15-ft) marble sculpture of the messenger goddess, Iris. Her wings outstretched, bedecked with precious jewelry and holding a metal herald's staff in her right hand, she seemed to hover on the column's capital, a conduit between heaven and earth. Her status – like that of Athens – was

trumpeted by an inscription running vertically between two of the column's flutings:

*Callimachus of Aphidna dedicated me to Athena –*
*I am the messenger of the immortal gods of Mount Olympus*
*– Callimachus, Athenians' War Archon, who fought*
*at Marathon for all the Greeks:*
*this monument is given by the sons of Athens.*

At Delphi, too, Athenians used victory as propaganda. They had already begun work on a treasury, strategically sited on a bend in the Sacred Way just yards north of the Siphnian Treasury, but thanks to booty won at Marathon they now reworked its design and the message it conveyed. At 9.8 × 6.7 m (32 × 22 ft), slightly larger than its Siphnian equivalent, and built from Parian marble, the **Athenian Treasury at Delphi** exuded a cool, Classical restraint, already far removed from the rococo excesses of its earlier rival. There were no caryatids here. Instead, topped by a gently sloping tiled roof, the clean lines of the side wall beside which visitors must walk led east to a shallow porch whose two central Doric columns supported the entablature, its proportions suggesting to the eye a perfect square topped by a shallow pediment.

On an Attic *kylix* (wine cup), c. 460 BC, a Greek hoplite attacks a fallen Persian.

A temple in miniature, the cool, Classical Athenian Treasury today bears replicas of its original metopes.

The sculptures that this pediment once housed are mostly lost, but fragments suggest their subject matter mirrored that of the great Temple of Apollo, towering on its nearby terrace – a god's arrival, this time not Apollo's into Delphi but Athena's on her chariot, perhaps reaching Mount Olympus. Like the temple, the treasury's west pediment contained sculptures showing the Gigantomachy, the battle now more than ever associated with Athenian democracy, since not only did it provide the foundation myth for the Panathenaic Festival (where the tyrannicides struck their blow for freedom), it served as a metaphor for Athens' victory over the 'barbaric' Persians. To stress which further, the western pavement of the platform (beneath the Gigantomachy) bore an inscription carved deep in proud capital letters: 'Athenians to Apollo from the first fruits of the Persians at Marathon.'

Both this inscription and the mirroring of the temple's pediments (financed a generation earlier by Athenians) spoke

to the growing confidence of Athens, as – to an even greater extent – did the treasury's metopes. Just over 66 cm (26 in.) tall and roughly 63.5 cm (25 in.) wide, each of these thirty sculpted slabs (six on the short sides, nine on the long) took as its subject matter the triumph of Greek civilization over barbarism, of order over chaos, and many showed exploits of the panhellenic hero Heracles. Today they are much damaged, and their specific location on the treasury cannot be known for certain, but among the scenes are Heracles' theft (or perhaps liberation) of the cattle of Medusa's grandson Geryon, and his killing of Cycnus, a highwayman who robbed from pilgrims going to Delphi, a scene which the sculptor, while retaining elements of Archaic art, such as the slightly orientalizing features of the hero, imbued with new vitality.

But especially striking was the subject matter of the remaining metopes. They showed episodes from the life of

On a now fragmentary metope from the Athenian Treasury, Theseus fights an Amazon.

Albert Tournaire's 1894 painting imagines offerings displayed outside the Athenian Treasury beside the Sacred Way.

another hero, this time an Athenian: Theseus. In the late sixth century, Athenians had been promoting the myth of Theseus; they had even commissioned an epic poem, the (now lost) *Theseid*; and they made much of claims by veterans of Marathon that they had seen both Heracles and Theseus fighting by their side against the Persians. But these metopes on the Athenian Treasury were the first time that the panhellenic hero and his Athenian equivalent had been shown in sculptures side by side as equals. Some of Theseus' triumphs echoed those of Heracles. Some metopes presented him cleansing the world of bandits and robbers; but others recalled him fighting off the Amazons when they invaded Attica (the legendary Amazonomachy), another myth that seemed to chime with recent history. One metope showed Theseus being greeted by Athena herself, the hero raising his right hand in greeting as he came into the goddess's presence, a stunningly audacious image, since, even though he was a king,

On another metope from the Athenian Treasury, Heracles captures the elusive Ceryneian Hind as one of his twelve labours.

Theseus was paradoxically being reimagined as the archetypal democrat, the epitome of the contemporary Athenian male. Furnished with heavy doors and strong metal grilles which barred access even to the porch, the treasury would in time be crammed with riches: gold bowls; bronze tripods; armour taken from defeated Persians; even the Archaic statues of Cleobis and Biton placed there by grateful citizens of Argos.

But just ten years after the Battle of Marathon it seemed as if the victory celebrations so implicit in the building might be horribly premature. In 480 BC, the Persians were back, their massive army and navy sweeping through northern Greece and the north Aegean down towards the mainland. So divided were the Greeks that, although faced with destruction, only thrity-one *poleis* out of many hundred formed a defensive alliance. Appeals to Sicilian colonists failed since they too were being attacked, this

The Serpent Column at Delphi consisted of a gold tripod supported on the heads of three intertwining bronze snakes.

time by the Carthaginians, whose strategy coordinated with Persia. Keen to regain kudos following their absence from Marathon, the Spartans sent a suicide squad on a fruitless mission to delay the enemy at Thermopylae, but soon the Persians had not only occupied Attica (most of whose population evacuated days before) but burned its temples in retaliation for the torching of the Temple of Cybele in Sardis nineteen years earlier. But the Greeks had a new weapon.

In 483 BC, Athenians discovered a new seam of silver in the mines at Laurium, with which they funded the construction of two hundred triremes, deadly warships designed for speed with a bronze-clad ram which could hole enemy hulls. With these, in the Bay of Salamis near Athens, the Greek alliance smashed the Persians' fleet, destroying their mastery of the waves and their supply lines. Once more the sea had come to the Greeks' aid. The next year, 479 BC, commanded by a Spartan, Pausanias, they routed the now-depleted Persian army at the Battle of Plataea, forcing its retreat to Asia Minor (modern-day Turkey).

To mark their victory, the allies set up trophies, the most significant of which was at Delphi. Here, opposite the altar and the Temple of Apollo, they erected a bronze column, 8 m (26 ft) tall, designed to represent three bearded serpents, each coiling round the other, tongues flickering from their gaping mouths, fangs bared, their heads supporting a huge golden cauldron. Funded by the tithe of spoils captured from the Persians at Plataea which had been set aside for such religious offerings, the **Serpent Column** should have been a monument to Greek unity in the face of existential threat, but when it was unveiled, its cauldron was found to bear the words: 'After defeating the Persians, I, Pausanias, the Greek general-in-chief, dedicated this monument to Apollo.'

Even the Spartans agreed it was outrageous to ascribe victory to one man, so the inscription was hurriedly replaced with 'Greece's liberators dedicated this when they freed their cities from grim slavery', while a list of the allied *poleis* was carved onto the column itself. However, this too provoked controversy, since the order in which they appeared implied a hierarchy. Naturally Sparta topped the roll of honour, but *poleis* such as Corinth and Aegina (both of which played a vital part in the war) might have expected to take second place. Instead, that went to Athens, a mark of her growing authority, while, as evidence of how power shifted, Mycenae came sixteenth, Naxos twentieth and Siphnos twenty-ninth.

A modern reconstruction of the sanctuary at Delphi shows the Temple of Apollo with a statue of the god beside it and the Serpent Column slightly below and to the right. It is instructive to compare this with the earlier reconstruction on pages 80–81.

Meanwhile, Sicilian Greeks were raising their own monuments to victory. In 480 BC, on the same day as the Battle of Salamis (or so it was later claimed), armies of the Syracusan tyrant Gelon and Theron, tyrant of Acragas, defeated Carthaginians besieging Himera on the north coast of Sicily, while a subsequent storm destroyed the fleeing enemy navy. Here, too, Greeks used a tithe from captured spoils to erect temples, the most ambitious of which was the **Temple of Zeus at Acragas**, a *polis* (on the site of modern Agrigento) famous for its wealth and flamboyant elegance. With money and labour no object – much of the workforce comprised Carthaginian captives – its architect let his imagination run riot. Theron had instructed him to site the building on a plateau between the city to the north and the sea to the south. Looking east beyond one of the main city gates, was a long ridge, where further temples would be built in the following decades; and west, beneath the cliff face, a vast pool was being constructed fed from pipes that drained off water from the local porous rocks. This was the so-called Colymbethra, a fishpond over 1,200 m (4,000 ft) in circumference and roughly 9 m (30 ft) deep, where locals gathered to admire the swans.

Below: C. R. Cockerell's 1830 reconstruction of the Temple of Zeus at Acragas imagines atlases or telamons positioned facing inwards within the *cella*.

Opposite: Set atop a ridge, the Temple of Zeus dominated the skyline of Acragas. Here, the atlases or telamons are shown between the exterior columns.

Opposite: C. R. Cockerell tries to suggest the scale of one of the atlases or telamons, which he imagines still standing amid the temple's rubble.

Above: Today's visitors can better appreciate their scale from a replica.

Facing a high altar, itself 54.5 m (179 ft) × 17.5 m (57 ft 6 in.), the 19.8-m (65-ft) tall Temple of Zeus occupied a massive five-stepped platform, 112.8 m (370 ft) long and 56 m (185 ft) wide, the largest of any yet conceived. While it is impossible to reconstruct its form with total accuracy, it is clear that with fourteen columns on the long sides and seven on the short (which meant there was no central door, but rather two at each edge), it was unconventional. It was also calculated to impress. While the columns surrounding the temple on all sides were so vast that a man could fit inside their fluting, perhaps because of the sheer weight of the roof they were not free-standing. Instead they were engaged into a half-height wall; and set atop this wall, between each column, were colossal statues, 7.5 m (24 ½ ft) tall. Sometimes referred to as 'atlases' or 'telamons', these were sculpted to represent alternately older and younger men, naked, their arms bent level with their heads, shouldering the burden of the entablature above him. Each outsized giant was a stand-in for a Carthaginian, defeated and enslaved and forced to support the temple to Greece's greatest god. It was a unique design, and one never repeated.

The Carthaginians' defeat was further celebrated on the building's east pediment, whose sculptures showed the Gigantomachy (a fitting subject to accompany the 'telamons'), and on the west by a scene from the Trojan War, in which (according to the Roman-era historian Diodorus Siculus' less than helpful description) 'each of the heroes may be seen to be portrayed in an appropriate manner'. Commonly paired in the Archaic Age, in the 470s BC this coupling of the Gigantomachy and Trojan War was assuming added significance. Now, as well as celebrating the victory of Greek civilization and order, it served as a useful metaphor for more recent victories over 'barbarians' (a shorthand term for those who did not speak Greek), whether they be Carthaginians or Persians. In fact, even the Persian Great King Xerxes seems to have viewed his invasion of mainland Greece as a continuation of the Trojan War. During his advance, he visited Troy to sacrifice at Athena's temple and pray for vengeance both for its mythical destruction and for the more recent burning of the Temple of Cybele at Sardis.

The roof of Acragas' Temple of Zeus was not intended to span the whole building. Like many other large-scale temples, its *cella*, here an aisle formed of two walls containing rows of square pilasters, would have been open to the sky – if the building had ever been completed. But it was not. It remained unfinished when, in 406 BC, the giants took their revenge. After an eight-month siege, the Carthaginians defeated Acragas, butchered many taking refuge in its temples, looted priceless works of art and destroyed much of the city.

It was a fate spared Syracuse, whose tyrant, Gelon, had similarly celebrated victory at Himera by constructing two monumental temples in the early 470s BC to essentially the same design. With a footprint of roughly 55 × 23 m (180 × 75 ft), and surrounded by regularly spaced Doric columns, six on the short sides and fourteen on the long, both consisted of a large *cella* flanked at either end by porches. Of the Temple of Athena Nike (Athena, Goddess of Victory), erected beneath Himera's acropolis on a five-stepped platform in a specially cleared sanctuary by the side of the river near where the Carthaginians were routed, only the foundations survive along with a few architectural details – not least a series of lion-head waterspouts, their bared fangs and lolling tongues reminiscent of the Medusa heads on the Temple of Artemis in Corcyra, but showing greater movement and plasticity. The pedimental sculptures are long lost, but fragments suggest that one set showed a familiar subject, the Gigantomachy, almost certainly highlighting

Looking north-west, the Temple of Athena (left) and the earlier, taller Temple of Artemis on Ortygia, Syracuse, are seen with Mount Etna in the distance.

Athena's role in killing the giant Enceladus (who legend said lay buried under Sicily).

Considerably more of the **Temple of Athena at Syracuse** survives, thanks to its being converted into a Christian church in the seventh century AD when much of its entablature and many of its columns were built into the new external walls. It was sited on the island of Ortygia, a long peninsula separated from the mainland by a narrow channel, which formed one side of the city's Great Harbour. Ortygia exuded exclusivity. Here stood not just the tyrant's palace but at least two earlier temples, the early sixth-century Temple of Apollo and a late sixth-century Temple of Artemis, and it was beside this on the site of another archaic temple, once adorned with running gorgons but now demolished along with neighbouring houses to accommodate a larger footprint, that the new Temple of Athena was built.

Left: Athena prepares to skewer the fallen, bleeding giant Enceladus on this sixth-century BC red-figure vase

Opposite: Syracuse's Cathedral incorporates the Temple of Athena's exterior Doric columns into its side walls.

While it, too, was decorated with lion-head waterspouts, there were differences between this temple and its sister at Himera. As befitted its location on Ortygia, Syracuse's Temple of Athena boasted huge doors faced with ivory and fitted with gold bosses, while its roof was made not from terracotta tiles as was the norm but from thin slabs of marble through which light would filter golden into the *cella* to bathe the statue of Athena in a celestial glow. Surviving fragments from the east pediment, which still bear faded paintwork, show how stunningly ornate the temple was: vigorous patterns decorate the corner of the cornice that once framed the central façade – meanders, leaves and flowers – their rhythm accentuated by their contrasting colours. There is no evidence that the pediments contained figurative sculptures, but it appears that onto one of them was fixed a massive gilded shield, which served as a beacon for sailors. Leaving Syracuse, voyagers would take with them an earthenware cup, which they would fill with flowers and honeycombs and spices, and drop it overboard when they were so far out to sea that they could no longer glimpse the sunlight glinting from the shield.

Back in the motherland, Greeks were celebrating their own victory over the 'barbarians' – as well as furthering old feuds

with one another. When a lightning strike damaged the east pediment of the **TEMPLE OF APHAEA** on Aegina in the Saronic Gulf some 27 km (17 miles) south of Attica, the islanders used the opportunity to install new sculptures vaunting their *soi-disant* position in the *poleis* pecking order, advertise a new-found patriotism and memorialize their past. In 490 BC, when the Persians first invaded, Aegina sided with the enemy, partly out of animosity for Athens, its economic rival, whose coastlines it regularly raided and whose growing power it viewed as a threat. But in 480 BC it switched sides. Now a staunch defender of Greek freedom, it was Aegina, not Athens, that was honoured by the allies for its key role in the Battle of Salamis, something that the islanders were determined to celebrate with new pedimental sculptures.

Sited on a mountaintop in the north of the island, with views across the sea to Attica, the Temple of Aphaea, dedicated to a local goddess linked to Artemis, had been built in 510 BC of limestone faced with gleaming stucco, its details painted in vibrant colours. Constructed on the cusp of the Classical Age, its partial use of the recently invented pulley meant that some columns could be formed of drums craned one on top of the other (others were monolithic), and within the airy *cella* a two-storeyed colonnade held up the ceiling. Like Syracuse's later Temple of Athena, this was made not of terracotta but thin marble tiles, which let light filter into the elegantly proportioned chamber. There, behind a wooden railing, two statues of the goddess stood side by side, one already ancient, the other a new incarnation. Meanwhile, the exterior was primped with sculptures: sphinxes crouched beside the lower corners of each pediment above whose apex tall-stemmed lotus flowers unfurled, each flanked on either side by statues of chic, stylish maidens.

As for the subject matter of the pediments, even in the late 500s it had been chosen to reflect the island's role in the legendary tales of Troy. The west side showed Ajax and his half-brother, Teucer, sons of Aegina's King Telamon, fighting in the war made famous by the *Iliad*. On the east was Telamon himself alongside the great panhellenic Heracles taking vengeance on Troy, when it broke a promise to the gods. But between each pair of heroes was another figure, larger and more powerful, dominating the design: Athena, orchestrating every movement, demonstrating her approval of the island and its heroic warriors. It was this scene which was damaged by the lightning strike, but rather than remove each sculpture and bury it in a pit (as was the norm when temples were destroyed by fire or earthquake), the Aeginetans

'AEGINA AND HER CITY ... IS LOVED BY ALL THE GRACES THANKS TO THE FAR-FAMED COURAGE OF THE AEACIDAE [TELAMON, AJAX AND TEUCER].'

PINDAR
*Pythian Ode 8*

Above: An Archaic sculpture of a heroically nude wounded hoplite occupied the left corner of the Temple of Aphaea's east pediment.

Overleaf: The Temple of Aphaea sits on a hill near Aegina's north-east coast overlooking the Saronic Gulf.

carefully preserved those pieces which were still intact and put them on display in a specially built exhibition hall within the sanctuary, deliberately memorializing them, self-consciously curating their own past.

In their place they installed fresh figures, full of motion and vitality. These were sculpted in the round, even though once in place their backs would not be seen (perhaps therefore a sign that prior to being hoisted onto their pediment they were briefly put on view beside their predecessors). They, too, showed the Trojan War, but this time with a bold new twist – the Trojans were represented wearing unambiguously contemporary Persian costume, not least trousers whose bold patterns were picked out in paint. While other artworks drew subtle parallels between mythology and recent history, Aegina's latest monument was unequivocal: the recent Persian Wars were a continuation of the Trojan War, and Aegina had shone in both. Indeed, even victory at Salamis was thought to be in part down to the spiritual intervention of the heroes Telamon and Ajax, since relics said to be their bones (which in peacetime

were kept in a shrine at Aegina town on the west side of the island) had accompanied the fleet into battle.

Talismans like these were central to Greek thought, and few were as powerful as the ancient olivewood statue of Athena which Athenians took with them from her temple before the Persians overran Attica. But now, it had no temple in which it could be housed. For a combination of religious, political and economic reasons, the Athenians had decided not to rebuild any temple burned during the war – even Athena's venerable olivewood statue stood in a makeshift shack on the Acropolis. The decision did not preclude the building of entirely new religious monuments such as a city-centre hero shrine for Theseus, whom veterans of Marathon swore they had seen fighting by their sides, and whose bones were miraculously (and conveniently) 'discovered' shortly after the Persian Wars. But as the decades passed, Attica's lack of prestige temples began to rankle, especially

Above: C. R. Cockerell's reconstruction shows the Temple of Aphaea's Archaic east pediment with acroteria of lotus flowers flanked by maidens.

Overleaf: Even in Hellenistic and Roman times, the Temple of Zeus dominated the sanctuary at Olympia.

**'YOU JOURNEY TO OLYMPIA TO GAZE UPON THE STATUE OF ZEUS, AND EVERY ONE OF YOU WOULD CONSIDER IT A GREAT MISFORTUNE TO DIE WITHOUT EVER SEEING IT.'**

EPICTETUS
*Discourses*

when relatively humble *poleis* were causing tongues to wag by building increasingly impressive temples of their own.

The most impressive of all was at Olympia. This panhellenic sanctuary was owned and run by Elis, an otherwise unexceptional state which came into sudden riches in 472 BC when it defeated a neighbour in battle. It decided to use some of its newfound wealth to build a temple, but not in Elis, in Olympia, where it could impress visitors from the entire Greek world taking part in the four-yearly Games. Moreover, by dedicating it to Zeus, Elis would for the first time give the festival's presiding god a temple of his own. Its location at the very hub of the Altis (the sacred precinct), close to Zeus' altar where vast numbers of animals were sacrificed, was chosen carefully.

Necessitating a major redevelopment of this part of the sanctuary, including the removal of many earlier artworks, the **TEMPLE OF ZEUS AT OLYMPIA** was the most impressive temple yet to be constructed on the Greek mainland. Within four decades it would also house the stunning statue of the seated god, described by many as a wonder of the world. Built of stuccoed poros stone (like Aegina's Temple of Aphaea), equipped with two deep porches and towering 20.7 m (68 ft) tall, the temple stood 70 m (230 ft) long and 29 m (95 ft) broad on a three-stepped platform with seven columns on each short side and thirteen on each long. Two further rows of seven columns divided the *cella* into three aisles, supporting the rafters and in turn the roof, constructed from one thousand translucent slabs of marble from Mount Pentelicus in Attica.

Marble (this time from Paros, easier to carve) was also used for the sculptural decorations. There were twelve metopes, six above the east porch, six above the west, each showing one of the labours of Heracles. Despite their mythological subject matter – a multi-necked snake, a three-bodied giant, a three-headed dog – they already hinted at the new plasticity and heightened realism that would characterize Classical art, abounding in compositional variety and even showing Heracles aging from one scene to the next. As well as being the all-Greek hero, and so ideally suited to be represented at the panhellenic sanctuary *par excellence*, Heracles had links with Olympia's prehistory, one of several figures connected to the Games' inauguration.

Another was the hero, Pelops, who gave his name to the Peloponnese ('the island of Pelops'). His already ancient tomb-sanctuary, the Pelopion, adjoined the temple, and preparations for his chariot race (in which, albeit by unsporting means, he would defeat and kill the local king and thereby win his daughter's hand in marriage) formed the subject of the great east pediment above

the *cella* doors. Like many Greek works of art, it showed a moment on the brink of action: here, the quiet lull before the race began, the two contenders each flanked by their chariots and horses and onlookers (all with some stake in the race), with, central to the composition, Zeus himself, the god who owned the temple. Despite the inactivity, the sculptor managed to convey a sense of tension. Knowing that they would melt during the race, Pelops had bribed a chariot technician to fit wax linchpins to his rival's wheels, and he is shown on the pediment as an old man recoiling in horror as he contemplates what must ensue. Shown, too, are personifications of the local rivers, Alpheus and Cladeus, near whose convergence the Altis was sited, a clear indication from the sculptor that the race was said to have begun here, where the temple stood.

If the figures on the east pediment still showed traces of Archaic stiffness, on the west pediment the sense of movement and vitality was tangible. This showed the Centauromachy. Fanning out on either side, the drunken, violent centaurs are first seizing local women before falling, struggling to their knees, attacked by vengeful Greeks, the whole scene fitting perfectly within the gradually diminishing space. Through the sophistication of execution and design, not least the use of unexpected diagonals and the varied sightlines of each character, the sculptor achieved a vivid sense of chaotic motion, which served to throw into heightened focus the central figure in the composition: the young Apollo, positioned beneath the apex of the triangle, larger than the rest, heroically nude, full frontal, handsome, his head turned, face impassive, right arm outstretched to quell the fighting. Even in fragments, and with its paint long gone, its power remains palpable. No wonder that at the Olympic Games of 456 BC, when the building was consecrated, Athenians were captivated, especially since their own Theseus took part in this myth that celebrated punishment of blasphemous wrongdoers. Within a few years they would be vaunting it on temples of their own.

In 449 BC, following defeat in Cyprus, the Persian Great King Artaxerxes signed a peace treaty not with the Greeks but with Athens on the Greeks' behalf. For the Athenians, this recognition of their kudos marked an important moment, while the peace dividend allowed them to reallocate resources from the military to public works. For thirty years they had left the temples burned during the Persian Wars in ruins, powerful reminders of all that they sacrificed for Greece. All they had done was fortify their city, ringing it with walls and building the Long Walls that linked it to its port of Piraeus, 6 km (3 ¾ miles) distant, a secure corridor

**'THESE WERE THE MOST POWERFUL MEN WHO EVER LIVED, AND THEY FOUGHT WITH THE MOST POWERFUL ENEMY, THE CENTAURS OF THE MOUNTAINS, AND DESTROYED THEM UTTERLY.'**

HOMER
*Iliad*

Centaurs make off with Lapith women on the west pediment of the Temple of Zeus at Olympia.

through which imported food could be brought up from the sea in the event of siege. Now, though, inspired by the peace treaty, Athens' leading politician, Pericles, invited every other *polis* to Athens to attend a panhellenic conference. Sparta refused, putting paid to the proposal, but Pericles had made his point: Athens could now claim to be the hegemon of Greece.

A new era had begun, and to mark it the city would embark on a new programme to replace many of the ruined temples. As project manager, the Assembly chose Pheidias, a sculptor already responsible for a number of patriotic installations including a 'Marathon Monument' at Delphi (thirteen bronze statues of gods and heroes near the start of the Sacred Way) and a 9-m (30-ft) helmeted statue of Athena Promachus (Athena Who Fights in the Front Line) on the Athenian Acropolis complete with spear and shield embossed with scenes from the Centauromachy. Both involved Pheidias in managing teams of artists, artisans and labourers, but neither was as ambitious as this new undertaking.

At the centre of the entire scheme was a 12-m (40-ft) tall chryselephantine (i.e. faced in gold and ivory) statue of Athena, triumphant, her right hand outstretched, a winged Victory alighting on her palm. Eye-wateringly expensive, it would take almost a decade to craft. To house both it and the earlier olivewood statue, the Athenians built what they called simply 'the Temple' or 'Hundred-Footer', but which today we call the **Parthenon** ('the Maidens' Temple', an enigmatic name perhaps referring to the virgin Athena and the local heroine Pandrosus), siting it beside the charred foundations of the Archaic Temple of Athena Polias (Athena of the City State), burned in the Persian attack.

Designed by the architects Ictinus and Callicrates and completed in 432 BC, the Parthenon was arguably the jewel in the crown of Greek architecture, and its setting on the Athenian Acropolis displayed it to perfection. No detail was overlooked – from the stylobate floor's subtle curvature to the columns' entasis – each swelling just 4.1 cm (1 ⅝ in.) in centre – to their subtle inward inclination, which meant that, were they to be

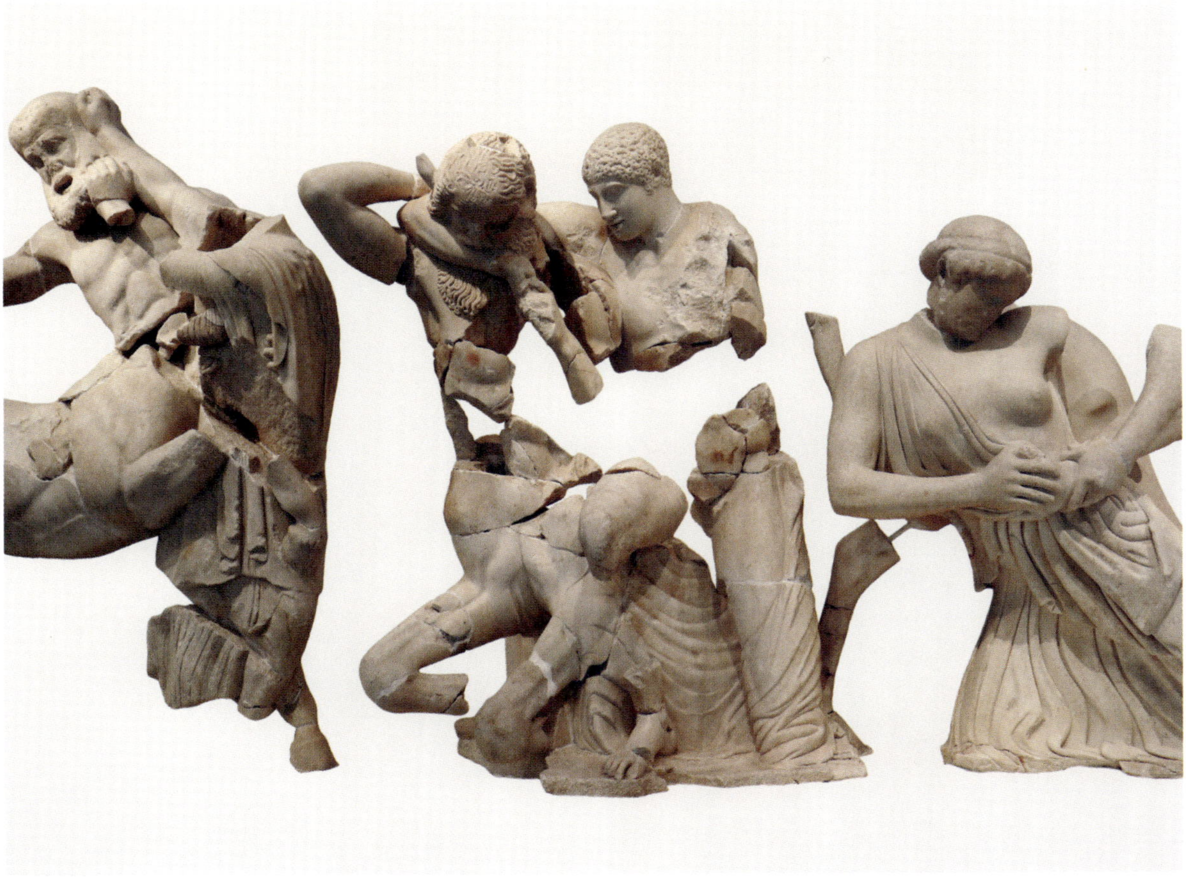

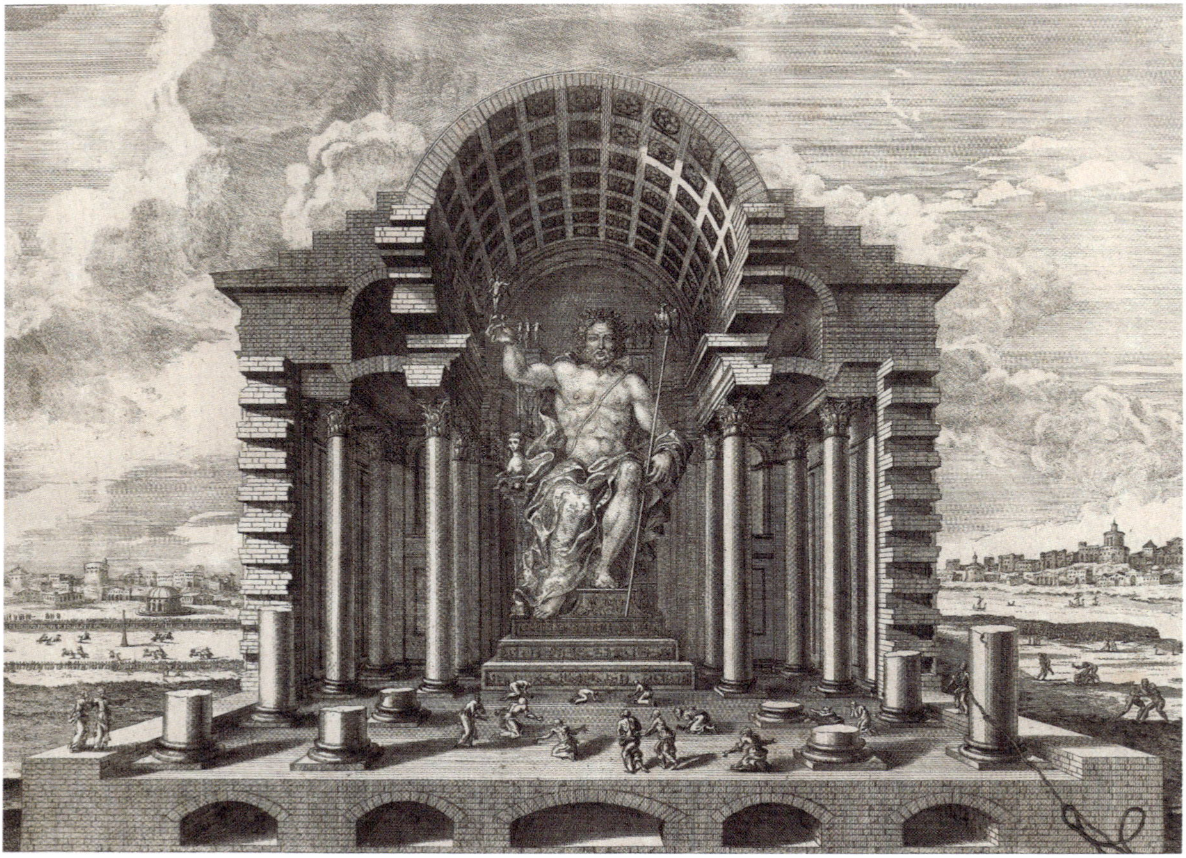

Opposite: This early eighteenth-century woodcut accurately conveys the scale of Pheidias' statue of Zeus at Olympia but misleadingly places it beneath a vaulted ceiling.

Below: Dominating the interior of the Parthenon, Pheidias' statue of Athena was calculated to inspire awe and wonder.

Overleaf: The Parthenon was the most richly decorated temple on the Greek mainland as Alexis Paccard's 1845 reconstruction of its east side well conveys.

extended, the seventeen columns on each of the two long sides would meet 2 km (1 ¼ miles) over the Acropolis, with the eight columns on the short sides meeting 5 km (3 miles) above the earth. Because the building was intended to showcase the statue, two tall windows flanked the massive door (itself faced in ivory and gold), through which the rising sun's rays poured into the *cella*, while light filtered, aureate, through the marble roof tiles. Within the *cella*, two rows of two-tiered columns flanked the nave with another running laterally behind the statue to add to a sense of spaciousness. In the *opisthodomos*, effectively a strongroom housing the empire's treasury, the ceiling was supported by four soaring columns, their capitals carved in a newly ornate style, pioneers of the Corinthian order.

The Parthenon was the most richly decorated of any mainland temple. Lotus leaves thrust upwards from the apex

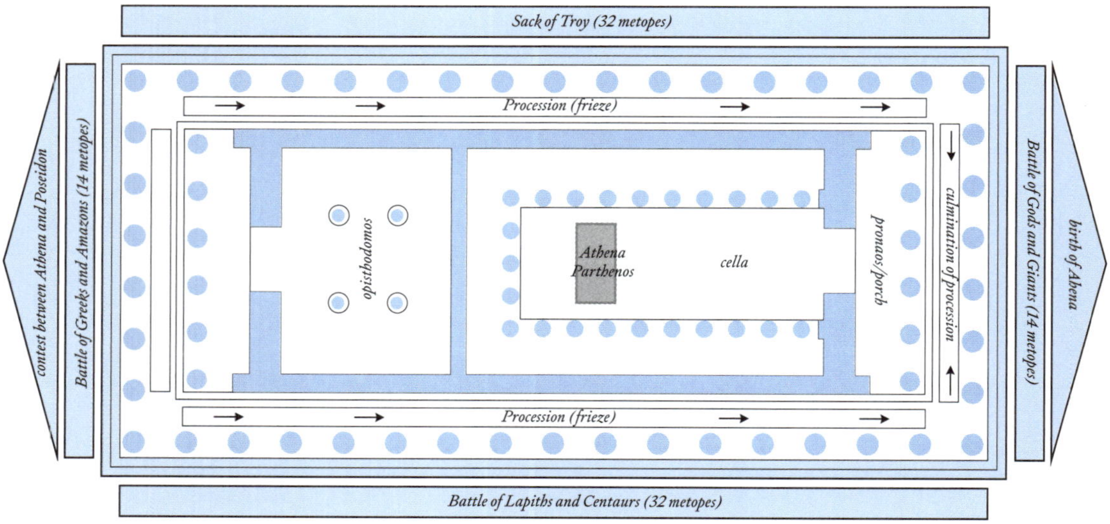


of each pediment, while winged Victories seemed poised to launch themselves from every corner. A Doric frieze of metopes embraced the building, each side showing scenes of struggle ending in Greek or Athenian victory: the Amazonomachy on the west and the Centauromachy on the south, both battles in which Theseus played a leading role; the Trojan War on the north; and on the east the Gigantomachy. All drew parallels with the recent Persian Wars, and with the exception of the Trojan War they were repeated on the statue's shield or sandals.

But if the Parthenon was a victory monument, it was also a celebration of the city's relationship with Athena, and the pedimental sculptures (carved in the round like those on Aegina's Temple of Aphaea) showed two episodes from her legendary life. On the east was the scene immediately following her birth, when, aided by the blacksmith god Hephaestus and observed by all the other gods, she sprang fully formed from Zeus' head, the composition with its swirling drapery brilliantly capturing the moment's energy. Meanwhile, the west pediment, its protagonists with their chariots and horses flanked by local river gods (rooting it firmly in the geography of Athens) showed Athena's contest with Poseidon to decide which of the two should own the land of Attica. This was a key moment in Athens' legendary history, and one confirmed by 'tokens' visible on the Acropolis (an olive tree believed to have been planted by Athena, a well they said had been created by Poseidon's trident).

Top: A plan of the Parthenon shows the positioning of the sculptures and statue.

Above: This 1845 reconstruction of the Parthenon's entablature shows an episode from the Centauromachy on a metope flanked by triglyphs.

Horsemen, one wearing a distinctive 'Thracian' cap, take part in a cavalry display, from the Parthenon's north frieze.

High on the *sekos*' outer wall behind the architrave a third sculpture element ran round the building, a low-relief Ionic (or continuous) frieze, 160 m (525 ft) long, 1 m (3 ft 4 in.) high, and at most 7.6 cm (3 in.) deep. Starting at the west side (the side seen first by anyone who accessed the Acropolis), then peeling off so it continued east along the north and south long sides, for the most part it showed a procession: men preparing to mount horses, before trotting, galloping, then reining back; armed men, or *apobates*, competing in a race involving leaping off a speeding chariot; musicians; sheep- and cattle-wranglers; and worshippers bearing urns and offerings. On the east side girls and women appeared, advancing towards the space above the *cella* doors. But now the mood changed drastically, for here sat the twelve Olympian gods arranged in two groups, while between them five mortals (two adults and three children) apparently performed rituals.

The frieze's meaning has been long debated. Most people accept an eighteenth-century interpretation that it shows the

A watercolour reconstruction of sections of the Parthenon's north and east friezes includes part of the cavalry display and chariot procession as well as musicians, sacrificial animals and the Olympian gods.

Panathenaic Procession in honour of Athena. However, there are too many anomalies (not least the presence of all twelve gods), and it is more likely that it represents the 'ideal' of a procession, in which Athenians leave the here-and-now of Athens (the first scenes, like the Amazonomachy and contest of Athena and Poseidon, all on the west side of the temple, are set on or near the Acropolis) before coming into the otherworldly presence of the gods (the Gigantomachy and Birth of Athena on the east side, too, take place in a cosmic realm). Other details, including the enigmatic central ritual scenes, suggest that contemporary Athenians may have understood the frieze to show their city's (and perhaps their own) transfiguration thanks to their sacrifices in the Persian Wars, with death leading to rebirth and a newly heroic status.

The theme of the Athenian as hero was explored on another temple conceived as a companion to the Parthenon. Known today as the **HEPHAESTEION** (or sometimes, wrongly, the Theseion), the Temple of Athena and Hephaestus was built on a low hill above the Agora. Begun just before the Parthenon, it had no dedicated workforce. Instead, builders and sculptors were moved between it and other projects according to demands, which meant that the temple was not finished until 415 BC, more than thirty years after it was started. Unusually, too, its design was generic, shared by no fewer than three other contemporary buildings, though the setting of each made them seem individual: the Temple of Poseidon at Cape Sunium, the Temple of Nemesis at Rhamnous and the Temple of Athena and Apollo at Pallene (a building which the Roman emperor Augustus would later move in its entirety to the Athenian Agora and re-dedicate to the war god, Ares). With six columns on their short sides – 13.7 m (45 ft) long – and thirteen on the long sides – 31.7 m (104 ft) long – and porches east and west but no back room, all were workmanlike, but what distinguished the Temple of Hephaestus were its sculptures.

These were a veritable monument to the Athenians' perceived uniqueness. Myth told how Hephaestus ejaculated on Athena's thigh; the goddess wiped herself with wool and threw it on the ground; and from the earth was born a boy, Erechtheus, from whom all Athenians believed they traced their ancestry. Athena and Hephaestus, then, were 'family', and the idea of family and location dominated both pediments. The east (overlooking the administrative and mercantile heart of Athena's city and out to her Acropolis) showed Athena's birth, while the west (facing the industrial Ceramicus district) showed the blacksmith god, Hephaestus, returning from temporary exile to be welcomed back to the embrace of Mount Olympus. Family and nurturing were

The Temple of Athena and Hephaestus was the first temple begun in the mid-fifth-century BC Athenian building project.

celebrated, too, on the acroteria at each pediment's apex, where sculptures carved in the round showed Hephaestus' nurses (the nymphs Thetis and Eurynome) accompanied by winged Victories. Within the *cella*, the base of the gods' statue was carved with the scene of Erechtheus' birth.

The temple was also a monument to Athenian democracy. Eight of the eighteen sculpted metopes showed Theseus, the proto-democratic king of Athens (the others showed the labours of Heracles). His victories – and his city's – were celebrated on the Ionic friezes high on the interior of each porch. The west frieze showed the Centauromachy, the east a battle between Theseus and other Greeks (perhaps his cousins the Pallantidae, who tried to overthrow him), observed by Zeus, Athena and the other gods and perhaps inspired therefore by the treatment of the Trojan War on the Siphnian Treasury at Delphi. They proclaimed the well-worn message of order triumphing over chaos, here honed specifically to show victory over both external enemies (the centaurs/Persians) and those closer to home (fellow Greeks or non-democratic Athenians). But what made the friezes extraordinary was Theseus' stance, for on each his posture mirrored that of one of the tyrannicides from their statue nearby in the Agora – the west copied Harmodius' stance; the east, Aristogeiton's. This was a daring departure for Greek monumental art, since it identified two recently dead humans with a demigod. Moreover, in Greek religion a hero must have one divine parent. Theseus' father was Poseidon. But, if Athenians could trace their parentage back to Hephaestus, did that not mean that they were in a very real way heroic, too?

The perennially appealing idea that people could somehow transcend their mortality or at the very least enjoy a happy afterlife had for centuries been central to the Eleusinian Mysteries, one of the festivals promoted under Peisistratus. These Mysteries – named from the Greek word for an initiate (*mystes*), but mysterious in our sense, too, because anyone revealing what happened at the arcane ceremonies faced dire punishment – assumed even greater significance following victory at Salamis, since Eleusis was sited on the adjacent coast, the battle took place at the time of the festival, and gods worshipped there were believed to have helped the Greek fleet. Chief among those gods were Demeter, the grain goddess, and Kore, her daughter, known also as Persephone, who was abducted by Hades, god of the Underworld, and returned to

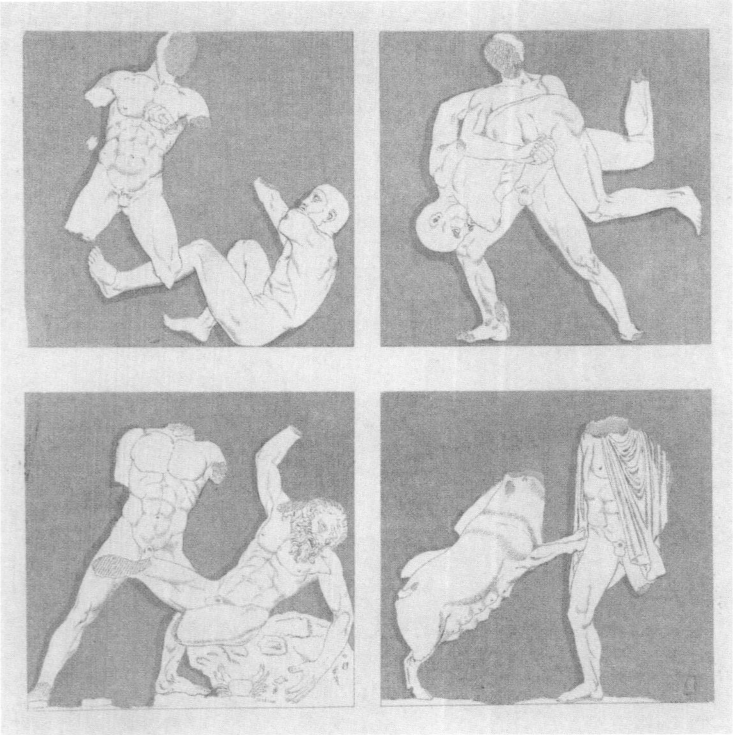

Below: Drawings from James Stewart and Nicholas Revett's 1794 *The Antiquities of Athens* show some of Theseus' adventures on metopes from the Temple of Athena and Hephaestus.

Opposite: On the west frieze of the Temple of Athena and Hephaestus, Theseus (centre) fights in the Centauromachy, mirroring Harmodius' stance from the tyrannicide statue.

earth only when her mother caused the crops to fail for so long that the continuation of human life (and thus sacrifices to the gods) was threatened.

Since Persephone had eaten pomegranate seeds during her captivity, she was compelled to return below the earth each year, but Greeks believed that she re-emerged into the light every September at Eleusis, and it was this moment, pregnant with significance for the agricultural year and fraught with hope for some kind of human resurrection, which seems to have formed the climax of the Mysteries. Following sacrifices and purification rites, a procession of 19 km (12 miles) from Athens to Eleusis, and rituals designed to disorientate and terrify (perhaps including ingesting a psychotropic drink), initiates appear to have witnessed a sacred drama where Persephone appeared in a blaze of torchlight with promises of postmortem pleasures – and it was this event that took place in the **TELESTERION AT ELEUSIS**.

By 449 BC, so many people – men and women, slaves and free – from across the Greek world were being initiated (an economic plus for Athens and a chance to project soft power), that the Telesterion built under Peisistratus and upgraded in the early years of democracy needed to be enlarged. That building had been 26.8 m (88 ft) square, with twenty-two interior columns supporting its tiled roof. At 51 m (167 ft) square, the new version, intended to accommodate no fewer than three thousand initiates, would be almost four times as large. Such a vast indoor space called for an ingenious design. A first plan involving twenty internal columns and a central lantern window rising above the inner sanctum from the 15-m (50-ft) high ceiling was soon abandoned, but, if anything, its successor was even more ambitious and more striking. Two storeys high, it kept its enlarged footprint but now made use of forty-two internal columns arranged in seven rows of six. While these undoubtedly affected the sightlines of initiates, many of whom were crowded on the eight shallow steps that ran around the walls, this apparently was not a major consideration. In fact, it was probably deliberate, since the rites relied not on reason but on pure animal emotion. Drugged, exhausted and confounded by a cacophony of shouts and clashing cymbals, worshippers saw and heard hidden snatches of what they were assured was the divine, and the blazing torchlight that accompanied the final revelation seems to be the moment that they most remembered.

The impact of Eleusis and the Telesterion was felt in Athens too. Also in 449 BC, an Odeon, or concert hall, was built on the southern slope of the Acropolis next to the Theatre of Dionysus. Like the Telesterion it was essentially square with a roof that rose sharply to a central apex 19.8 m (65 ft) high and an external colonnade, which took its entire footprint to a mighty 62 × 69 m (205 × 225 ft). It, too, required a forest of internal columns, ninety in total, but here these were made of wood – reputedly the masts of Persian ships captured at Salamis. Indeed, the entire building was a monument to victory, said to be modelled on a massive tent captured following victory at Plataea. The tent had served as the Persians' headquarters and was believed by many to have belonged to the Great King himself. The internal columns were not the only wooden element: to produce the best acoustics the entire interior was built of polished wood.

Choosing the right building materials was important not simply for their architectural properties, but for their spiritual significance as well. The Eleusinian Telesterion was made from dark blue-grey limestone, which, being local, played a crucial part in the myth associated with the Mysteries – it was through this limestone that Persephone was thought to ascend to earth each year – and Eleusinian limestone was thought to contain such sacred potency that it was incorporated into many of the buildings and sculptures at this time. Statues such as the chryselephantine

**'GARLANDED, [THE INITIATE] STRIDES OUT WITH A NEW FREEDOM ... CELEBRATING HOLY RITES, CONVERSING WITH PURE, HOLY MEN.'**

PLUTARCH

The fourth-century BC Ninnion tablet imagines initiates to the Eleusinian Mysteries with Demeter and Kore.

Opposite: A reconstruction of the Athenian Acropolis shows the ramp leading up to the Propylaea with the Parthenon beyond.

Below: A 1794 plan of the Propylaea demonstrates its asymmetrical design. The Temple of Athena Nike is on the bastion (bottom right).

Overleaf: Leo Von Klenze's 1846 painting, *The Acropolis of Athens*, imagines the view from the nearby Areopagus hill with Pheidias' statue of Athena Promachus rising above the Propylaea.

Athena in the Parthenon stood on a base of Eleusinian limestone, and soon it was being built into the very fabric of two new constructions on the Athenian Acropolis.

In 437 BC the Parthenon's structure and statue had been completed, Pheidias had departed for Olympia to construct his huge chryselephantine Zeus, and no further consignments of building materials needed to be hauled up onto the Acropolis. Work therefore began on the great entranceway, the **PROPYLAEA**. This was the structure through which every visitor to the Acropolis must pass, not only affording security for treasures housed within the Parthenon but also acting as a spiritual portal onto the sacred rock. This religious aspect was underscored by the use of Eleusinian limestone which ribboned round the top of the two bastions on either side of the main gateway, continued as the lowest course of its great central hall, and formed the top step of its inner flight of stairs.

The site of the Propylaea presented major challenges, not only because the ground was desperately uneven but also because it contained visible remains of earlier Bronze Age structures which the Athenians wished to preserve. Moreover, the brief given to the architect Mnesicles was not just for a gateway, but a complex which would include rooms and halls on either side, commanding the entire west face of the plateau. He responded with great vision. His first decision concerned its orientation. While the previous gateway had faced south-west, Mnesicles rotated his new

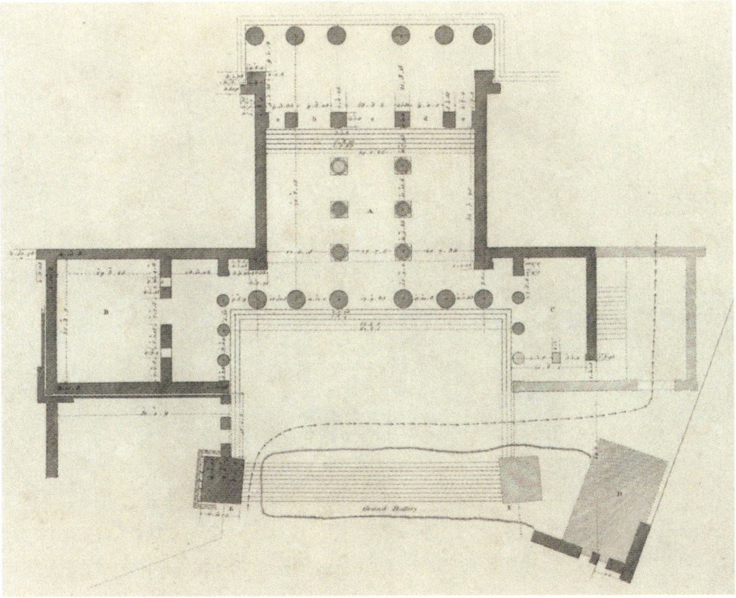

building's axis slightly northwards both to ensure a perfect alignment with the Parthenon and so that, looking out, its central doors would frame the distant hills of Salamis, a reminder of victory over the Persians. His second decision was subtly to mirror the architecture of the Parthenon itself. Both façades of the gateway, towering high atop the rock and approached via a zigzagging ramp, were narrower versions of the temple's east side, this time with just six Doric columns, supporting an entablature with trigylphs, blank metopes and a pedimented roof. Each gave onto a porch. Particularly impressive was the outer, western porch or hallway, its roof supported by six Ionic columns, painted a deep vibrant blue and studded with gold stars – a cosmic stage-set heralding the gates themselves. There were no fewer than five gates in all: a massive central doorway (through which the Panathenaic procession made its way each summer) flanked by

Today steps replace the original ramp up to the partially reconstructed Propylaea.

'IF ATHENS [WERE TO BE ABANDONED], HER APPEARANCE WOULD SUGGEST THAT SHE WAS TWICE AS STRONG AS SHE REALLY IS.'

THUCYDIDES
*History of the Peloponnesian War*

four narrower entrances, their height stepping down slightly from the centre, all hung with heavy wooden doors.

The north wing housed two large halls for state banquets and a public art gallery where paintings (on wooden boards) might be displayed. It was also faced in polished Pentelic marble, as were the two bastions between which rose the ramp onto the rock. Special thought was given to the southern bastion, whose Bronze Age wall was still in good condition. Loath to conceal this link with what Athenians believed to be an age of heroes such as Theseus, when Mnesicles clad the bastion in marble, he incorporated windows through which to view the ancient masonry. More problematic were foundations of a Bronze Age building discovered on the proposed site of the Propylaea's southern wing, which would need to be destroyed if Mnesicles kept to his original plan. Instead, he abandoned it. So potent was this archaeology that, like the remains of the Archaic Temple of Athena Polias a little to the east, they were left untouched, a potent monument to the past.

By 432 BC, the Propylaea was close to completion. All that remained was to remove some lifting bosses, around which ropes were tied for craning marble blocks, and which were usually smoothed off once the stones were into position. But suddenly work stopped. It would never be resumed. Athens had become embroiled in an expensive war, first with Corinth, then with Corinth's allies led by Sparta. Called today the Peloponnesian War, it would drag on until 404 BC, involving most of the Greek-speaking world from Sicily to Asia Minor, and ending only when Sparta, now backed by Persia, forced Athens, exhausted, divided and deprived of vital food supplies, to surrender. Persia was not the only foreign power to profit from Greek disunity. Returning to Sicily, the Carthaginians defeated much of the west of the island, including Acragas, where they even massacred those seeking refuge in its temples. In Greek eyes this was impious, but already Athenians had been forced to confront their own relationship with gods. At the start of the Peloponnesian War, a plague struck Athens, killing around a third of its entire population. At the same time, heavy rains destroyed crops, leading to famine, while major earthquakes brought down or damaged buildings – including the recently consecrated Parthenon, where part of the east front was cracked and sculptures dislodged. Perhaps encouraged by the oracle at Delphi, Athenians feared that they had somehow displeased Apollo (among other things, the god of plague), Poseidon (god of earthquakes) and their own patron, Athena. In 425 BC they responded by building new temples.

Chief among them was a new Temple of Athena Polias on the Acropolis, designed to supersede the Parthenon as home to the goddess's revered olivewood statue. Like its predecessor, burned by the Persians, it would consist of an east-facing *cella* and a series of chapels dedicated to other gods and heroes, including Poseidon and the mythological king alongside whom Poseidon was worshipped – Erechtheus. It is from him that the building takes its name today: the **Erechtheum**. The existence of the Propylaea now made it less easy to bring building materials onto the Acropolis, but even more problematic was the temple's proposed location. Because most of the plateau already housed temples or sanctuaries of other gods, and because the ruins of the old burned temple were so sacred that Athenians could not build over them, the only remaining site lay between these ruins and the north edge of the plateau, where the ground shelved so steeply that the east

Opposite: The entrance to the Erechtheum's back rooms were through the north porch, while to the west a false façade rose above the Garden of Pandrosus.

Right: A ground plan of the Erechtheum shows its unusual design.

Below: On a fifth-century BC Athenian vase, Athena receives the baby Erechtheus from the earth-goddess, Gaia.

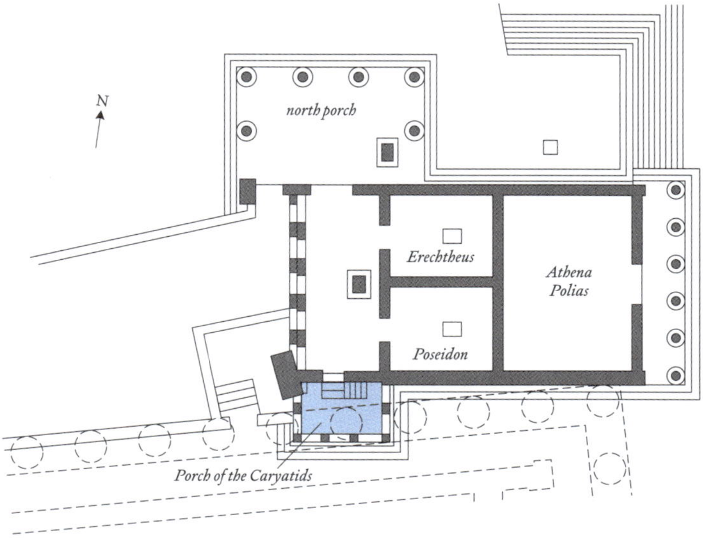


side was ten feet higher than the west. One architect was already experienced in overcoming such difficulties – Mnesicles, whose Propylaea exuded confidence and harmony. Once more, he rose to the challenge.

Rather than flatten the ground by creating an artificial terrace, which would have interfered with not only the garden housing Athena's sacred olive tree but important Bronze Age graves, Mnesicles built the temple on two levels, so that the floor of the *cella*, with its porch of six Ionic columns and its east wall studded with two windows, was higher than that of its western rooms. Here, too, he made bold decisions. Topography meant that there could be no west porch or door, so Mnesicles moved both round to the north, where an imposing porch gave on to an inner hall, illuminated by windows on the western wall, and leading through to the two chapels of the *opisthodomos* (one of them dedicated to Poseidon and Erechtheus), and on to steps which climbed back upwards to the level of the *cella*. But this was not where they led. Instead, they opened onto a porch, the only part of the temple to encroach onto the foundations of old temple. Built over a grave supposed to belong to Cecrops, its intended function is unknown, but it was clearly intended to stand out dramatically from the rest of the building's blank south wall, since instead of columns, the porch's roof was supported by six statues of young women, today called caryatids. Their hair well coiffed and wearing long dresses hanging in graceful folds

down to their ankles, each of the carefully painted maidens carried a sacrificial bowl and gazed impassively across the sacred ruins to the Parthenon.

Like the Porch of the Caryatids, the entire temple was elegant. Unusually for such an important building, it was not peripteral, so Mnesicles ensured that its exterior was alive with sculptural detail. Round the top of the wall ran a continuous (Ionic) frieze not carved *in situ* like the Parthenon's but comprising individual marble figures or groups of figures fixed onto a band of spiritually potent Eleusinian limestone. Too few survive to tell what scenes they showed, but they are likely to have been connected to early myth, perhaps those involving Erechtheus and Poseidon. Beneath the frieze stretched dazzlingly painted garlands – alternating lotus blossoms and palmettes – whose theme was picked up at the top of every column shaft, which were themselves studded with sparkling glass and jewels.

If the temple was intended to appease Athena, it seemed to work. In 425 BC, almost immediately it was begun, the plague

Above and opposite: Replicas of caryatids gaze out from their porch on Athens' Temple of Athena Polias (Erechtheum), while drawings from Stewart and Revett's *The Antiquities of Athens* show how they were perceived in 1794.

stopped, and Athens' fortunes changed dramatically. An unexpected victory saw Spartan troops surrender for the first time in their history, an event which Athenians celebrated by hanging captured Spartan shields from the south bastion of the Propylaea and building on the confined space above them an exquisite **Temple of Athena Nike** (Athena, Goddess of Victory). The project had been in the planning since the mid-430s, but events had conspired to prevent its execution. Like the Temple of Hephaestus and Athena in the Agora, it followed a basic blueprint repeated in two other contemporary buildings: a temple for Artemis Agrotera (Artemis the Huntress) on the outskirts of Athens, in recognition of that goddess' help at Marathon; and a new temple for Apollo on Delos, housing seven earlier bronze statues now repositioned on a plinth of Eleusinian limestone.

Perched high atop the bastion as if on a tall plinth, which jutted westwards, 8.5 m (28 ft) above ground level, from the Propylaea complex, the Temple of Athena Nike was tiny, its footprint of 5.3 × 8.1 m (17 ft 6 in. × 26 ft 7 in.) even smaller than

the treasuries of both Athenians and Siphnians at Delphi. But its setting made it especially eye-catching. Even more pleasing was its design: two narrow porches, east and west, each with four Ionic columns 4 m (13 ft) tall supporting a shallow pediment; the *cella*, a mere 3.8 × 4.1 m (12 ft 5 in. × 13 ft 6 in.), in whose east wall two windows were inserted to illuminate the statue within; and the sculptural details of its pediments and Ionic frieze which ran around the entire building. Being a monument to victory, it was not surprising that many of these sculptures mirrored those of the Parthenon in showing scenes of battles. Thus the themes of each pediment were identical to those of the relevant metopes on the Parthenon, the east showing the Gigantomachy, the west the Amazonomachy, and while much of the frieze is too damaged to identify its subject matter, the action of the east frieze clearly involves gods, perhaps witnessing Athena's birth (the subject of the Parthenon's east pediment). In the other sections of the frieze are scenes of battles, but which battles it is difficult to tell. Not all are mythological: the south frieze shows Greeks fighting Persians (identifiable through weaponry and dress), and it includes one figure whose pose mirrors that of Harmodius in the tyrannicides statue. He may represent Callimachus, the Athenians' general-in-chief at Marathon, who, according to Herodotus, was urged before the battle to leave a legacy 'such as not even Harmodius and Aristogeiton left behind'. That he, like they and others who had sacrificed their

Above: A computer-generated image includes acroteria of golden Victories as well as the sculpted balustrade around the Temple of Athena Nike.

Opposite: Today replicas of its Ionic frieze adorn the partially reconstructed Temple of Athena Nike.

lives for Athens, was now considered a hero was indicated by his depiction fighting in a state of heroic nudity.

The extravagance of this vision was repeated on a balustrade constructed round the temple in 410 BC, following a series of unexpected victories that suggested Athens' fortunes were improving. Topped with railings and surrounding three sides of the bastion, this low marble parapet 41.8 m (137 ft) in total length, and just over 0.9 m (3 ft) high, was carved in medium relief with scenes showing Athena watching as winged Victories led bulls to sacrifice and built trophies out of Persian and Greek armour. The workmanship was so stunning that it has rightly been recognized as one of the highlights of Classical Greek art. Using a technique known as 'wet drapery', whereby clothing seems to cling to bodies to reveal the form beneath or slip suggestively from outstretched limbs, it imbued the composition – young women struggling to restrain bulls, or caressing captured shields, or captured in the moment as they tied their sandals – with a sensuality bordering on the erotic. This was a far cry from the realities of war, a decadent male fantasy of the fruits of victory. The temple's wooden statue of Athena (holding a helmet in her left hand to demonstrate that war was over and a pomegranate in her right to link her with the Eleusinian message of rebirth) has not survived. Later guides maintained it was in fact a statue of Victory – but wingless. The Athenians, they said, removed her wings to ensure that she could never fly away.

In fact, only a few short years after temple, balustrade and statue were completed, the Athenians were forced to accept Sparta's surrender terms, including the dismantling of their Long Walls to the sea which had enabled them to withstand siege so long as they ruled the waves. But the temples remained

Above: The Temple of Athena Nike's south frieze showed Greeks fighting Persians.

Opposite: A nineteenth-century photograph captures a winged Victory adjusting her sandal from the Temple of Athena Nike's balustrade.

untouched, monuments to what would be called Athens' Golden Age. Some Athenians admitted that their buildings overstated their real power, among them the historian Thucydides, who reflected that if Athens were to suffer the same fate as Mycenae, and lie ruined and depopulated, thanks to her temples, 'her appearance would suggest that she was twice as strong as she actually is'. The suggestion still persists today.

# THE FOURTH CENTURY BC

(404–338 BC)

THE FALL OF ATHENS was a profound moment in Greek history, but despite a brief period of civil turmoil, the Athenians quickly recovered – and, as they did, the kaleidoscope of inter-*polis* relationships shifted once more. Less than a decade later, they were again at war with Sparta, but this time with unlikely allies – their old enemies the Corinthians and Thebans. More unlikely still was the identity of Sparta's chief ally. He was Greece's old arch-enemy, the Great King of Persia, the price for whose support had been control of the Greek cities of Asia Minor. Soon even he tired of the Spartans, intervening on mainland Greece to impose a short-lived peace, whose terms were shattered in a clash of egos between Thebes and Sparta. By now, however, Sparta was in decline, no match for the new battle tactics of Thebes' strategists, and defeat at Mantinea in 362 BC saw her crushed.

Despite the almost constant turmoil, however, individual *poleis* and regions had continued to make their mark on the landscape by raising ever-more lavish and impressive monuments. Towards the end of the fifth century, the people of Argos, for so long Sparta's chief rivals in the Peloponnese, built a new temple for their patron goddess, Hera. Enjoying a commanding position at the edge of the plain north-east of the city, her sanctuary, the so-called **HERAION OF ARGOS** (to which Cleobis and Biton once dragged their mother in an ox cart) had attracted interest since Archaic times, when a massive terrace was constructed from huge boulders, their size deliberately paying homage to and rivalling those of nearby Mycenae's Cyclopean walls. Atop this stood a temple, roughly 56 × 34 m (183 × 113 ft), approached by a ramp from the south-east and with a fine paved

'IN EXECUTION, THE STATUE MADE BY POLYCLEITUS WAS THE MOST BEAUTIFUL IN THE WORLD'

STRABO
*Geography*

As imagined in this painting from 1902, the Heraion of Argos was a magnificent sanctuary complex arranged over several levels.

area to the west, on which statues and offerings were likely displayed, their glittering metalwork visible for miles. At some point in its history, this building was replaced, and two columned stoas were laid out side by side beneath it on a lower terraced platform, the western, at 61 m (200 ft), some three times longer than its neighbour. But in 423 BC the temple was destroyed by fire, when its priestess, Chrysis, accidentally left a blazing torch too close to a heap of garlands.

Rather than simply rebuild it where it stood, the Argives left the old site empty, like the Heraion's faux-Cyclopean stones or Athens' ruined Temple of Athena Polias a memorial to a bygone age, constructing its replacement in front of the two stoas on the lower terrace, approached now from the south by a broad monumental staircase. The population of Argos had been decimated by Sparta in the 490s BC, after it chose the wrong side of history by staying neutral in the Persian Wars, and it was barred from fighting in the Peloponnesian War by a peace treaty – but by the late 420s Argos was newly resurgent and keen to advertise its power, though it was not until the end of the fifth century that the temple was completed. Designed by local

Opposite: This imaginative reconstruction by Antoine Chrysostôme Quatremère de Quincy of Polycleitus' statue of Hera in the Heraion was published in Paris in 1815.

Below: This sculpture of two small birds, identified as cuckoos, was discovered at the Heraion. According to mythology, Zeus transformed himself into a cuckoo in order to woo Hera.

architect Eupolemus, it was Doric in style, though unusually with six columns on the short sides and only twelve on the long, and rose proud above limestone foundations, 40 × 20 m (130 × 66 ft), its stone *sekos* adorned with marble – Pentelic for the metopes and Parian for the roof tiles and pediments, sculptures whose subjects, writes Pausanias, included the birth of Zeus, the Gigantomachy and the Sack of Troy.

To show the sacking of a Bronze Age city was perhaps a clumsy choice, for the temple housed an ancient statue made of wild pear wood, which the Argives seized as booty from another sanctuary of Hera when *they* sacked the town where it once stood – the ancient settlement of Tiryns, a few miles to the south-east. Now, this venerable image was displayed beside a towering statue of the goddess seated on her throne. On her head she wore a crown worked with reliefs of Graces and the Seasons, while in one hand she held a pomegranate, symbol of rebirth, and in the other a sceptre on which perched a cuckoo, the bird into which her husband Zeus had once transformed himself to woo her. Magisterial in the temple's half-light the statue gleamed in gold and ivory, the work of another Argive, Polycleitus, who made painstaking use of measurements and mathematics in his search for artistic perfection. According to Strabo, in this Hera he achieved it. In execution, wrote the Roman-era Greek geographer, it was 'the most beautiful in all the world'.

It was not just Argos that attracted the best artists. Even during the Peloponnesian War, communities vied to hire the

most prestigious craftsmen, not least the remote *polis* of Phigaleia, which commissioned Ictinus, architect of Athens' Parthenon, to design a new **TEMPLE OF APOLLO EPIKOURIOS AT BASSAE** high in the mountains of Arcadia. Despite being wild, inhospitable and ringed by towering crags, the site had been a sanctuary for many centuries, complete with other shrines to deities including Artemis and Aphrodite, and home to at least three previous temples of Apollo. But in the early 420s BC, perhaps in gratitude to the god for some perceived assistance (*epikourios* means 'helper'), the Phigaleians commissioned a new building that surpassed them all. Crouching on a small plateau with views across the mountain ridges to the sea beyond, the temple dominated the landscape, a brooding giant, whose design enhanced its air of timelessness. Its *sekos* and columns were constructed from blue-grey local limestone, whose colour seemed to change from light to dark throughout the day, and its roof was dazzling white marble. 'After the temple at Tegea', wrote Pausanias, 'it may be placed first for the beauty of its stone and its harmony.' Yet that harmony was cleverly contrived.

Below: The ruined Temple of Apollo Epikourios at Bassae crouches amid the rugged mountains of Arcadia. Today it is covered by a massive canopy to protect it from the elements.

Opposite: Published in 1860, this section by C. R. Cockerell shows the inner chamber, frieze and statue of Apollo in the temple at Bassae.

Partly to accommodate an existing building, but also to create a great feeling of awe, Ictinus eschewed the Classical proportions of the Parthenon, blending the unconventional with the Archaic: it was long and narrow, 38 × 14.6 m (126 × 48 ft), with six columns at the front and rear, and fifteen on each side.

Unusually, the temple was aligned to face not east but north, perhaps because in winter, when Bassae can lie under heavy snow, Apollo was believed to migrate northwards to the 'Land of the Hyperboreans'. Even Delphi marked his absence at this time, its sanctuary consecrated for three months instead to Dionysus. With foundations cradled on a thin layer of clay and sand between 5 and 20 cm (2 and 8 in.) deep (an early example of seismic isolation, a protection against earthquakes), it boasted uncommonly bold architectural elements. Among these were the engaged half-columns that supported the inner *cella* wall, the single freestanding column topped (for one of the first times in history) by a Corinthian capital (identifiable from its exuberant acanthus leaves) that partly blocked access to a smaller inner chamber (perhaps a throwback to the sacred pillar that appears

Left: A section of the east frieze of the Temple of Apollo Epikourios shows a scene from the Amazonomachy.

Opposite: A computer-generated image shows the Temple of Asclepius, the *abaton* (ward) and *thymele* (or *tholos*) at Epidaurus' healing sanctuary.

in Bronze Age art such as Mycenae's Lion Gate), and this chamber's two spur walls that angled out into the *cella*. The inner chamber's function is unknown. Unusually, it featured a grilled window on the eastern wall, intended, it is speculated, to allow the rising sun's rays to illuminate the twice-life-sized bronze statue of Apollo that stood here in the temple for some decades before being relocated to the marketplace of nearby Megalopolis.

While the exterior of Ictinus' other masterpiece, the Parthenon, was ablaze with sculptures, the two pediments of Bassae's temple were left unadorned, and only at the front and rear were there carved metopes. Today they are too damaged to allow the myths they showed to be reliably identified. More easily distinguishable are the subjects of the temple's other set of sculptures, a continuous (Ionic) frieze that ran high around the inside of the *cella*. These combined two well-known battles, the Amazonomachy and Centauromachy, familiar not least from the Parthenon. Indeed, to a keen-eyed observer, even certain individual scenes would have appeared familiar, since their composition was clearly borrowed both from the metopes of that earlier temple and from the shield of its chryselephantine statue. But here in Bassae the execution on the whole was less sophisticated and of more uneven quality, evidence of a rag-tag team of sculptors, whose numbers may have ranged from three to nine, some of whom were capable of crafting virtuosic wet-style drapery, others who could churn out only soulless, lumpen pastiches of Athenian originals.

Among the more successful panels was one showing Artemis riding into battle on a chariot drawn by two deer, while Apollo stands beside her nocking an arrow. The artist uses the perspective of the chariot wheels and the folds of the gods' drapery to great effect. Bizarrely, however, it was set not central to the composition, where it might be thought to have belonged, but in an obscure corner at the north-west of the *cella*. This, together with evidence that many blocks (all of which, unlike the Parthenon's, are self-contained) were shortened after sculpting, suggests not only that the frieze was carved elsewhere before being set in place, but that the composition, once it was assembled, was not arranged as its creator had originally intended. What happened between drawing and installation cannot now be known, but a coherent sense of drama is curiously lacking.

The same could not be said of the **Asclepium at Epidaurus**. Set amid lush countryside in the north-east Peloponnese and controlled by the nearby seaside *polis* with which it shared its name, this sanctuary was originally sacred to Apollo, but over the course of the fourth century BC it was systematically transformed into a lavish, even grandiose religious centre dedicated chiefly to Apollo's son Asclepius. Myths told how, through observing the behaviour of snakes,

Left: Made from Pentelic marble, this now fragmentary statue, an embodiment of one of the breezes, once graced the Temple of Asclepius at Epidaurus.

Opposite: Another statue depicting an embodied breeze was shown beside a semi-recumbent horse.

Overleaf: Thanks to the genius of its architect, Polycleitus the Younger, the theatre at Epidaurus has perfect sight-lines and acoustics, which are still appreciated by audiences today.

Asclepius had learned not just the arts of medicine but how to resurrect the dead, in punishment for which Zeus killed him with his thunderbolt before granting him a place among the gods. By the late fifth century, he was recognized as a major healing deity, and his sanctuary at Epidaurus (near which he was said to have been born) became the largest on the Greek mainland.

At its heart were three constructions begun around 375 BC. The first was a Temple of Asclepius. Squatter than many of its predecessors – with six columns on the short sides, eleven on the long and no rear porch – it was made from limestone but included decorative elements carved from Pentelic marble and an inner colonnade with pillars whose capitals may have been Corinthian. Surviving accounts show that the project took a mere four years and eight months to complete, a vivid testament to the energy and zeal of both its architect, Thedotus, and those spearheading

Floral motifs adorned the coffered ceiling of Epidaurus' *thymele*.

the project to transform the sanctuary, men who would inscribe beside the doors, 'To enter this temple, heady with incense, you must be pure, and to be pure you must think holy thoughts.' They were also hard-headed businessmen, who did not lack funds. The temple's sculptures were magnificent: scenes of the Amazonomachy and Sack of Troy adorned the pediments; winged women, embodiments of breezes, their clothing fluttering behind them, rode or stood beside rearing horses on the acroteria; and enthroned in the *cella* sat a 6-m (20-ft) chryselephantine statue of Asclepius, with a serpent rising up beneath one outstretched hand and a dog lying at his feet – a nod to the many dogs that roamed the sanctuary, encouraged to lick pilgrims, since their saliva was believed to contain healing properties.

Part of Epidaurus' *raison d'être* was to serve as hospital-cum-sanatorium, and at the heart of this endeavour was the second

**'TO ENTER THIS TEMPLE, HEADY WITH INCENSE, YOU MUST BE PURE, AND TO BE PURE YOU MUST THINK HOLY THOUGHTS.'**

INSCRIPTION ON THE TEMPLE OF ASCLEPIUS

key construction. As part of their treatment, patients needed to prepare themselves both mentally and physically, make offerings to the god and perhaps drink drug-laced soporific potions before the process called 'incubation'. This involved spending the night asleep in a dormitory, where snakes slithered over them, Asclepius appeared in dreams and priests (or doctors) performed what we might think of as more conventional interventions. Separated from it by a narrow passageway, the *abaton* ('dormitory' or 'ward') in which this happened was sited next to the temple's long north side. In appearance it resembled a two-storeyed stoa, 36 m (118 ft) in length, with an Ionic colonnade facing out towards the temple and the broad courtyard behind it, which was perhaps the venue for cult rituals.

For this courtyard housed the third significant construction, known to the Greeks as the *thymele* (from *thyo*, 'I sacrifice'), but, like the circular Bronze Age tombs, sometimes called the *tholos* or 'rotunda', one of only three such round structures on the Greek mainland. Raised on three steps, with a diameter of 21 m (70 ft 6 in.), an external peristyle of twenty-six limestone Doric columns, and a marble roof, the interior could be accessed, like all buildings at Epidaurus, by a ramp. But while the façade – with its colourfully painted floral metopes, its rosette frieze and flowery coffers – was elegant and beautiful, the inside opened out into another world. It was furnished with a circular colonnade of fourteen intricately painted Corinthian columns and walls adorned by panels by the encaustic artist Pausias of Sicyon (including one showing Eros laying down his bow and picking up a lyre, and another a drunken woman draining a crystal goblet, through which her face was clearly seen) – but its most distinctive feature was its floor. This was paved with highly polished black-and-white rhomboid slabs, with, at their centre, a circular stone which could be lifted up to reveal a chamber below. This was a narrow circular room divided by stone walls into three concentric corridors, linked by partially blocked openings which meant that anyone who accessed them was forced to zigzag back and forth as if in a maze. The purpose of the *thymele* is now unknown, but it may have been intended as Asclepius' cenotaph, where votaries could enact their own descent into the underworld before being raised again, in the same way that patients undergoing incubation underwent a deep sleep similar to death.

It was not the only enactment that they would experience. Since one of ancient medicine's key tenets was 'a healthy mind in a healthy body', Epidaurus was provided with three venues for further nurturing the physical and spiritual: a gymnasium, an impressive stadium and a theatre. Perhaps for the first time in theatre architecture this structure, designed, like the *thymele* by Polycleitus the Younger, featured a circular *orchestra*, 20 m (66 ft) in diameter and a rectangular stone stage building, which would eventually become two storeys high. Raked seating wrapped around more than half of the *orchestra* and was later extended to accommodate an audience of 12,000 to 16,000, when the 34 lower rows, arranged in 12 wedged sections, were augmented with 21 upper rows in 22 wedges. In a breathtaking understatement, Pausanias remarked that it was 'well worth seeing', before adding that it was unequalled in its symmetry and beauty. The product of meticulous mathematical and architectural calculation (its measurements are perfect to 10 cm (4 in.), using the limestone of the seating to supress lower sonic registers, and an interplay of three circular zones to reflect the higher tones back to the audience, its acoustics remain unrivalled.

Circles were becoming fashionable. Around 370 BC another circular temple was constructed, the **THOLOS OF DELPHI**, not

Below: The *tholos* in the Sanctuary of Athena Pronaia at Delphi blended traditional motifs with daringly innovative architecture.

Opposite: The sculptural decoration of the Tholos of Delphi included scenes from mythology, a ribbon of foliage and lion-head waterspouts.

Overleaf: A modern reconstruction sets the Sanctuary of Athena Pronaia with its *tholos* in context of Delphi as a whole, with the Temple of Apollo rising on the hill beyond.

in Apollo's sanctuary itself but beneath the cliffs in front of it, an area sacred to Athena, where in consequence she was worshipped as Pronaia, 'Before the Temple'. It was a site of special numinosity to Greeks, especially Athenians, since, according to folk memory, it was here in 480 BC that invading Persians were driven back by showers of rocks that crashed down from the mountain. They thought this showed Apollo's wrath; more likely, it was an earthquake. Already by the late sixth century BC seismic activity had destroyed an early Temple of Athena constructed on a sturdy terrace a hundred years before. Around 510 BC it was replaced by a new building (perhaps with money from the same Athenians who had recently funded the completion of the Temple of Apollo) and adorned with sculptures of Athena and flying Victories. The constraints of its location meant that both this temple and the new *tholos* faced south.

Daring in its design, exquisite in its execution and sumptuous in its sculpted decoration, the *tholos* was a magnificent fusion of diverse architectural styles and raw materials. Just over 14.7 m (48 ft) in diameter, and raised on three shallow steps, its exterior comprised twenty Doric columns supporting an architrave, with a band of sacred Eleusinian limestone topped by forty Parian marble metopes exploring those favourite subjects of Greek sculpture the Centauromachy and Amazonomachy in high relief. Above these ran a further band of Eleusinian limestone capped by a marble ribbon of riotous foliage from which lions' heads jutted out above each intervening triglyph. Eight dancing female figures

ringed a marble roof, whose appearance remains controversial: opinion is divided as to whether it was conical or octagonal or even domed.

The layout of the interior is more certain. Beneath a coffered ceiling and set on a paved floor of white marble with a border of Eleusinian limestone, a low bench ran around the walls, from which rose ten engaged half-columns, confidently Corinthian, supporting a Doric frieze whose subject may have combined battles involving Theseus and Heracles with a scene showing an assembly of gods. Their now fragmentary state makes details of the composition hard to tell, but the skill and technique of their sculptors is beyond doubt.

Like the *tholos* at Epidaurus, a question mark hangs over the purpose of this building. Writing that its architect, Theodorus of Phocis, penned a treatise on its design, the Roman Vitruvius describes it as a 'vaulted temple' in his *On Architecture*, but he may have been mistaken, or by the first century BC it may have changed its use. Pausanias does not mention it at all, which is surprising since – whatever its intended function, whether as a hero-shrine, a chapel to a chthonic deity, an armoury, a trophy raised in thanksgiving for victory, or a temple for Athena – it was one of the most delicate and graceful monuments in the entire Greek world.

Elsewhere on mainland Greece other projects were underway – though on a considerably larger scale. Following his defeat of Sparta in 371 BC, in an attempt to neutralize his enemy, the Theban general-cum-politician Epaminondas founded the elegant new city of Messene in former helot heartlands in the foothills of Mount Ithome, while further north up to forty communities all moved to Megalopolis (as its name suggests, a 'big city', equipped with one of the largest theatres on the mainland), another significant new conurbation aimed at resisting Sparta should she ever rise again. But while both these settlements enjoyed fine constructions and broad streets, no individual building in either mainland Greece or the Greek west (where Sicily was facing existential threats from her old rival Carthage) could match the sheer scale and ambition of a monument erected in Asia Minor in what had been till recently (and would soon become again) a Greek city on the coast of Caria.

The **Mausoleum at Halicarnassus** was (in all senses of the word) extravagant. Greek in style and influence and designed by one of the Greek world's leading architects, it was commissioned as a tomb for Mausolus, the Persian local

While there is no general agreement about what the Mausoleum at Halicarnassus looked like, this reconstruction presents one possibility.

These colossal statues, which once embellished the Mausoleum at Halicarnassus, have been identified (without firm evidence) as Artemisia and her brother Mausolus.

governor (satrap), by his sister Artemisia, who, following the custom of their family, was also his wife. Overlooking the sea, it stood in pride of place on a terrace in the centre of their newly redesigned and rebuilt city, where it might be seen most clearly. In their former capital, Mylasa, Artemisia had already helped plan the lavish burial of her father, Hecatomnus, in a finely painted sarcophagus adorned with portrait sculptures, but her ambitions for her husband were on an altogether greater scale. Upon his death in 353 BC, she tasked the Greek architect Pythius with constructing a monument more visually arresting than any that his world had ever seen, a testament to Artemisia's great grief and her great fortune, and though she died just two years later, laid to rest beside her brother-husband, the work continued to its completion.

But what did it actually look like? Toppled in an earthquake, its stones and sculptures pillaged, little remains, and Classical descriptions are frustratingly imprecise. In one section of his *Natural History*, the Roman Pliny describes it as being '63 feet

> **'[THE MAUSOLEUM] SURPASSED ALL OTHER MEMORIALS TO THE DEAD IN NOT JUST SIZE BUT BEAUTY.'**
>
> LUCIAN
> *Diologues of the Dead*

long on the north and south sides, shorter on the other two, with a total circumference of 440 feet, rising to a height of 25 cubits and surrounded by 36 columns.... Above the colonnade there is a pyramid, its height equal to that of the lower part, contracting by twenty-four steps up to the top, where is a marble four-horse chariot, the work of Pythius. Including this, the entire construction is 140 feet tall.' Modern scholars have suggested a multiplicity of reconstructions, but apart from its essentially tripartite construction (podium, colonnade, pyramidic roof), today's scant remains, including foundations excavated deep into the bedrock, are tantalizing in their ambiguity.

However, we can be fairly certain that three bands of friezes encircled the building: one, nearly 0.9 m (3 ft) high, crowned by egg-and-dart moulding and forming the podium's upper course, showed a vibrant Amazonomachy; the second, which may have run around the plinth beneath the chariot, depicted a Centauromachy; and the third, whose position is unknown, included racing four-horse chariots. These were not the only architecturally embedded sculptures. A row of lion-head spouts capped the colonnade; the coffers of the ceiling that the colonnade supported were adorned with battle scenes in low relief; but of even greater note was the forest of free-standing statues that gazed out at the viewer from all four sides of the construction.

Some, showing Persians and Greeks in battle, were life-sized; others, nearly 2.4 m (8 ft) tall, were of standing figures wearing local Greek or Persian dress; others still, at almost 3 m (10 ft) tall, depicting scenes of hunts or sacrifices as well as portrait statues (including two said to be Artemisia and Mausolus – the face is similar to one shown on Hecatomnus' tomb) may have stood between the columns. And then there were the massive marble lions. Exactly where the statues were positioned is debated, but once more Pliny gives a flavour of their brilliance. For involved in their creation were some of the greatest artists of their day: Scopas, who would soon provide sculptures for the Temple of Artemis at Ephesus; Bryaxis, who also provided a statue for nearby Cnidus; Timotheus, who had worked on the Temple of Asclepius at Epidaurus; and Leochares, of whom we shall hear later. Vitruvius, too, lists them, though with one important difference. In place of Timotheus he names Praxiteles, a master of plasticity, whose lifelike Aphrodites won great admiration.

Partly because of our inability to recreate the Mausoleum and partly because it was subsequently listed as one of the seven

wonders of the ancient world, it continues to intrigue popular imagination, but this should not blind us to its revolutionary importance, for there are some things we can say with certainty. In its bid to outdo all earlier freestanding funerary monuments (only the Bronze Age Treasury of Atreus, which is subterranean, comes close in its ambition) it blended Greek and non-Greek elements in a way and on a scale never before seen. As the Roman-era satirist Lucian observed, it 'surpassed all other memorials to the dead in not just size but beauty, with horses and men sculpted most perfectly in the best marble'. Further, it was made to honour not a city or a god but a powerful man, and as such it caught the spirit of its age. For across the sea in northern Greece there ruled another powerful man, who also memorialized his ego, who would soon defeat all Greece, and whose son would go on to transform the Greek and wider world forever.

Philip II had seized the throne of Macedon in 359 BC, and within just over twenty years, thanks to his ruthlessness, shrewd politicking and military flair, he had enlarged his kingdom to include not only much of Thrace (parts of modern-day Bulgaria, Turkey and north-eastern Greece) but mainland

Above: Conceived by the same architect as the Mausoleum at Halicarnassus, the royal Palace at Aegae, with its imposing façade, commanded the surrounding town and countryside.

Opposite, above: Discovered at Aegae (modern Vergina), this fourth-century BC ivory carving has been identified as representing King Philip II.

Opposite, below: The ground plan of the Palace at Aegae reveals its grand design conceived around an expansive central courtyard.

Greece. A century and a half earlier, one of his predecessors, Alexander I, had been forced to undergo a humiliating investigation to prove his Greek credentials in order that he might compete at the Olympic Games, but in more recent years virtuosic Greek artists such as Zeuxis and writers such as Euripides had flocked to the wealthy Macedonian royal court. So, when Philip ordered the building of a new **Palace at Aegae**, Macedon's ancient capital, it was no wonder that the illustrious Pythius, architect of the Mausoleum at Halicarnassus, should be commissioned to design both it and the associated complex that included both a theatre and religious sanctuaries.

While its design mirrored that of a conventional private house, the palace, nestling beneath a fortified acropolis, was conceived on a quite epic scale – appropriately for a kingdom that Athenian sophisticates accused of sharing many Bronze Age elements. With an area of around 15,000 sq. m (161,500 sq. ft), it was the largest building of the Classical Greek world. Its façade was simple yet revolutionary. In essence it resembled a two-storeyed stoa, 88 m (288 ft) long, with columns supporting the first floor and (above a band of triglyphs) Ionic columns holding up the terracotta roof. These colonnades housed a public area with spaces for discussion, desks for clerks and even wooden boards on which to publish judgments and decrees. At the heart

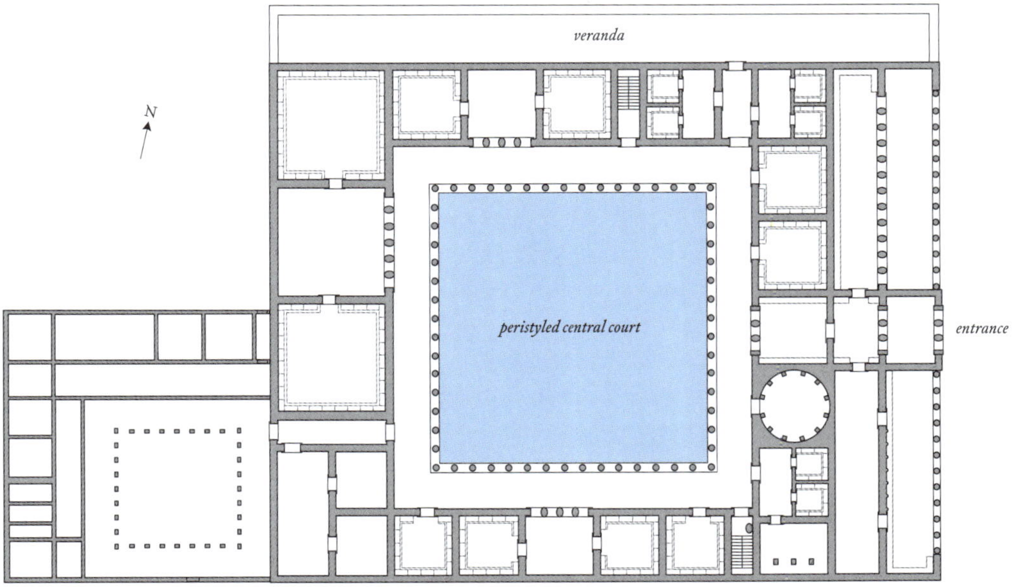

of this façade, however, slightly off-centre, was a monumental gateway, also two-storeyed, distinguished by its slightly protruding side walls and pediment. Here a pair of Ionic columns, taller than the Doric columns of the 'stoa', flanked massive doors, while on the register above them were six pseudo-windows. The building clearly had a great impact on those who saw it. Its façade was even reproduced in that of a tomb (the Tomb of Judgment) at nearby Mieza.

Through the imposing doors, a vestibule with long galleries on either side led first into a square antechamber furnished with desks on either side then through into a central square courtyard, 3,995 sq. m (43,000 sq. ft) in area, the hub of the entire complex. Surrounded by a portico supported by sixteen Doric columns, 7.6 m (25 ft) tall, on every side, it could accommodate eight thousand people, a place of assembly, where king and subjects might meet and interact. From here, too, the layout of the palace

The façade of the Tomb of Judgment at Mieza, which today preserves some of its paintwork, was modelled on that of the Palace at Aegae.

'[PHILIP] INHERITED A MACEDONIA ENSLAVED TO THE ILLYRIANS, BUT MADE IT MASTER OVER MANY PEOPLES AND THEIR CITIES.'

DIODORUS SICULUS
*Library*

became immediately clear: the east wing with not just its gateway and administrative offices but a round chapel dedicated to Philip's declared ancestor Heracles; the residential south wing with its suite of banqueting halls, each adorned with sumptuous mosaics, some interspersed with intertwining flowers, one showing Europa's rape by Zeus transformed into a bull (perhaps an allegory for Philip's own ambitions); the west wing which included a ground-floor suite comprising two reception halls, at just over 279 sq. m (3,000 sq. ft), the largest yet without internal columns, linked by a vestibule (with the potential to seat upwards of five hundred people), and an annex with a further (single-storey) peristyle and service rooms; and the north wing where a corridor gave access to a narrow terrace running the entire length of the palace with views across the theatre and the city towards the rolling plains beyond.

Faced with stucco to resemble marble, utilizing a rich wealth of stones, adorned with fine mosaics and paintings, furnished with exquisite bronze and marble statuary, and adhering in its geometry to the Pythagorean 'golden ratio', the palace proclaimed not simply Philip's power but his sophistication, undisputed Hellenism – and ambition. Indeed, at the same time, across the shallow Thermaic Gulf, builders were hard at work on yet another palace complex near the busy port of Pella, Macedon's commercial hub. This was a city of broad boulevards and rigid grid design, with an agora 7 hectares (17 acres) in area, rich houses boasting fine pebble mosaics, and temples dedicated to the Greek goddesses Demeter and Aphrodite as well as to the Anatolian Cybele.

Aegae and Pella both exude enormous confidence, and even for contemporary Greeks (for all that they might have sneered at Macedonians as uncouth northerners) it must have been clear that the balance of power was shifting away from the traditional centres of Athens, Corinth and Thebes. All doubt was eradicated in 338 BC, when on the Boeotian plain Philip's well-drilled army defeated an alliance of mainland Greeks at Chaeronea. Soon afterwards, a monument, the **Lion of Chaeronea** was erected on the battlefield. A full 6 m (20 ft) in height, the marble statue sat bolt upright on a podium: proud, muscular, with deep-set eyes and shaggy mane, gazing out across the scene of recent carnage.

But whom or what did it commemorate? Pausanias was in no doubt. 'Nearing the town', he wrote, 'you see the mass grave of the Thebans who were killed in the struggle against Philip. There is no inscription, but atop it is a lion, no doubt in

Opposite: With its geometric patterns and lush plants with coiling tendrils, this mosaic adorned a floor of the Palace at Aegae.

Above: Dating from around 320 BC, this mosaic from Pella shows young men identified as Alexander (left) and his companion, Hephaestion, preparing to despatch a lion.

recognition of their fighting spirit. The reason for this lack of an inscription is, I think, because their bravery was not equal to their fortune.' The Thebans in question were members of the Sacred Band, a crack regiment of three hundred heavily armoured soldiers, made up of pairs of lovers. Formed around 379 BC, it was wiped out here at Chaeronea and poignantly, when the enclosure round the statue was excavated, 254 of their skeletons were found laid out in seven rows. Which begs another question: since the Thebans and the other mainland Greeks had been defeated, why did Philip let them raise such a conspicuous and arguably defiant monument? The answer must be that it suited his own propagandist purposes. Such was the reputation of the Sacred Band that its destruction added kudos to his victory, while the fact that the surviving Thebans were obliged to conduct burial rites and raise a monument at their own expense on the site of their defeat added insult to already painful injury. For, while it was a grave marker, the Lion served simultaneously as a trophy of Macedonian victory, erected where the battle turned in Philip's favour, close to the cremation site of his own fallen, above whose ashes he erected a great tumulus. Ever sensitive to symbolism, by graciously allowing the Thebans to honour their dead, he was in fact ensuring that their monument would stand for future generations as testimony to his subjugation of the Greeks.

This was the message of another monument that Philip himself caused to be erected at this time to mark the dawning of

Opposite: A photograph from 1914 shows the monumental lion, restored just over ten years earlier, erected to commemorate the Theban dead at the Battle of Chaeronea in 338 BC.

Below: Lion-head waterspouts such as this one were set into the guttering of the Philippeion at Olympia.

Overleaf: This reconstruction drawing shows the sanctuary at Olympia at the confluence of the rivers Alpheus and Cladeus, with the stadium and hippodrome to the right, the Temple of Zeus in the centre and the Temple of Hera beyond it to the left. The Philippeion is immediately in front of the Temple of Hera.

his new world order – only this memorial was yet more controversial, a constant aggravating unavoidable reminder planted with deliberate unsubtlety at the sacred heart of the old panhellenic world. The third of Greece's three rotundas, the **PHILIPPEION** was sited at the entrance to the Altis at Olympia, yards away from both the venerable Temple of Hera and the Pelopion (the walled-off enclosure sacred to the hero Pelops), and in clear sight of the Temple of Zeus. With a diameter of 15 m (50 ft), its eighteen Ionic columns of Pentelic marble topped with a stone entablature with lion-head guttering, and its sloping marble roof crowned with a shimmering bronze poppy head, it rose some 10 m (33 ft) tall from a three-stepped marble base. A south-facing door gave access to the interior, with its flagstone floor (rhomboids describing sections of a circle) and nine engaged Corinthian columns appearing dazzling white against red-plastered poros (a type of limestone) walls. Two windows pierced these walls, and through these and the door the midday sunlight poured onto statues set opposite the entrance on a curved marble podium. Like Pheidias' celebrated Zeus, the

Opposite: A plate from Ernst Curtis and Friedrich Adler's *Olympia* of 1896 shows a cross-section of the Philippeion and details of its floor.

Below: Minted toward the end of Philip II's reign, this four-drachma piece shows on one side the head of Zeus and on the other a jockey on a prancing horse above an olive crown. This, together with the inscription 'Of Philip' suggests it is commemorating his victories at Olympia.

king of gods and men, that glittered in its nearby temple, these statues, too, were faced in gold and ivory, the work of one Athenian-born Leochares (whose work already graced the Mausoleum at Halicarnassus). But shockingly none of the statues were of gods. Instead, they were of members of the Macedonian royal family: Philip; his parents, Amyntas and Eurydice; his wife, Olympias; and his son Alexander.

Again, the message or, rather, messages were clear. Five generations earlier, Olympic bureaucrats had patronized a king of Macedon by questioning his Greek ethnicity. Now his descendant, Philip, victor in the Olympic horse race of 356 BC, in the Olympic four-horse chariot race of 352, and the Olympic two-horse chariot race of 348, was exerting his right to raise a victory monument in the Altis – to mark not only victory in these equestrian events, but victory in battle over all of Greece. Elegant, sophisticated, quintessentially Hellenic like the royal Palace at Aegae, in its design the Philippeion was a perfect distillation of centuries of previous Greek architecture. But its intention was to turn the old world on its head. Aligned neither to the sunrise nor the sunset but to the sun at its noon zenith, it declared that it was neither a temple nor a sanctuary of a dead hero. Rather it was a shrine for living demigods, a dynasty who through their deeds on earth deserved to be depicted as the true heirs of Olympian chryselephantine Zeus. Greeks who traced the progress of ideas from the *Iliad*, in which doomed Achilles is destined to become immortal, to the overblown and ostentatious tomb of Mausolus, the Hellenizing satrap, might have concluded that the Philippeion marked the logical next step on the warlord's path to self-deluded grandiosity. But most are likely to have shared a more immediate conclusion, articulated pithily by the Roman writer Justin, more than half a millennium later. 'For all Greece', he wrote, defeat at Chaeronea – and by extension the building of the Philippeion to commemorate it – 'marked the end of Greece's glorious supremacy and ancient independence'.

Except that he, and they, were wrong. The Greek world would change. But it would still stay (relatively) free for three more centuries.

# IV.

# THE HELLENISTIC AGE

# THE GREEK WORLD OF ALEXANDER

(336–31 BC)

KING PHILIP II OF MACEDON died in 336 BC, cut down by an assassin as he entered the theatre at Aegae to preside over an opulent political and religious ceremony. Hastily, his estranged wife, Olympias, and sidelined son, Alexander, seized the reins of power, executing any deemed to be a danger, including Philip's new wife Cleopatra Eurydice (his kingship let him take twelve wives) and newborn child. Whoever was behind the coup, protocol dictated that Philip receive a state burial, and his funeral was one of the most lavish ever seen. Attended by his army and his subjects together with his family and the elite of Macedon and wider Greece, it drew inspiration from Homeric epic.

Likewise, the layout of his tomb (whether wittingly or not) reflected the royal *tholos* tombs of the Bronze Age: a *dromos* cutting through a mound towards a monumental façade from which a doorway led into a chamber, this time two-roomed, rectangular and with a vaulted ceiling. The cremation itself took place atop the mound, the tall pyre formed of wood and mud bricks, crowned by a wooden building, intricately carved and painted to resemble Philip's palace or perhaps his tomb. In this, the body, dressed in armour, its head wreathed by a gold oak-leaf diadem, was placed upon a gold and ivory couch and surrounded by rich offerings before the entire edifice was torched. The king was not alone. To accompany his journey to the underworld, his hunting dogs and horses, too, were slaughtered, while a young Thracian princess, another of his wives, committed suicide rather than survive him. And so, with Cleopatra Eurydice and her baby, they were laid to rest within the tomb, while athletic games were held in the king's honour.

With painted decorations including a vivid hunting scene, Tomb II, one of the jewels of the Royal Necropolis at Aegae, was for many years identified as belonging to Philip II of Macedon.

Fifty years later, Philip's tomb, along with three others in the **Royal Necropolis at Aegae**, was covered with a huge grave-mound that helped preserve it. So, when they were excavated in the 1970s it was discovered that, while two tombs had been looted, two had not. Among these the façade of 'Tomb II' is especially impressive: a marble door flanked by half-engaged Doric marble columns, with two further pilasters and a wide entablature distinguished by its vibrant paintwork: blue triglyphs, terracotta bands and a remarkable scene spanning the whole building that shows a royal hunt apparently including portraits of both Philip and Alexander. The composition, possibly the work of Philoxenus of Eretria (an artist known for his speed, whose later depiction of the Battle of Issus has been immortalized in a mosaic), was finished only hours before the tomb was covered with its first mound (the paint was not yet dry when earth was shovelled) and does show signs of haste. Another artist famed for speed was Nicomachus of Thebes, and it is likely that he was responsible for a painting dominating an inner wall of the tomb of Philip's mother, Eurydice. This striking depiction of Hades' rape of Persephone shows the god driving a red chariot pulled by two white horses, clutching the maiden as she tries to flee, her gold hair and purple dress billowing behind her, as Hermes runs ahead. The myth was shown, too, on a gilded and painted marble throne discovered in the tomb, its iconography reflecting teachings of contemporary mystery religions, in which the purifying fire of the cremation helped prepare the dead to meet the rulers of the Underworld. Further wall paintings have been found in the necropolis showing chariot racing, a seated mourning woman and young men standing guard, which, together with the scrap of cotton tunic, purple-dyed, found in Tomb II, serve as provocative reminders of a wealth of lost artworks and textiles.

Among the profusion of treasures buried in Tomb II – including four sets of ornate armour, a chryselephantine shield, couches decorated in gold, ivory and glass, a wooden bed adorned with plaques of ivory, a fine bronze lantern, silver cups and jugs, a gold *fibula* (buckle) and chain – is a box, or *larnax*, almost 48 cm (19 in.) long, almost 33 cm (13 in.) wide and 20 cm

Below: Painted on the inner wall of the tomb of Philip's mother, Eurydice, this depiction of Hades' rape of Persephone is notable for its vigour and vibrant colours.

Opposite: Among the treasures discovered in the royal tombs at Aegae was this gold crown of oak leaves and acorns, symbols of Zeus.

(8 in.) tall, made of 24-carat gold and weighing 11 kg (24 lb). Its lid is embossed with a sun emitting sixteen rays, the symbol of the royal house of Macedon. Discovered in a marble chest, it contained a gold wreath intricately decorated with oak leaves and acorns, together with partially cremated remains. When discovered these provoked excitement, since wounds to the skull and one leg seemed to chime with written records to confirm that they belonged to Philip II, an identification that has since been questioned.

Even as Philip's remains were being interred, there were questions about whether his successor, Alexander, really was his son. Olympias, the young man's mother, claimed that his father was in fact none other than Zeus himself, something that the new king did little to deny. Within a few years he was sweeping through Asia Minor at the head of a Greek army, 'liberating'

Left: This silver *alabastron* jug from Tomb II at Aegae from 336 BC is decorated with heads of Heracles wearing his lionskin.

Opposite: An imaginative print of Ephesus made around 1725, before the temple was rediscovered, includes insets of the reconstructed building and statue of Artemis.

Greek cities from Persian rule before driving the Persians from Egypt and conquering their entire Empire. Passing through Ionia he found work already underway on a new **Temple of Artemis at Ephesus**, since in 356 BC (on 21 July, to be precise) its predecessor had been burned down (by an arsonist, Herostratus, intent on winning immortal fame). Legend soon had it that the only reason that the goddess let her temple be destroyed was that she had been distracted by Alexander's birth on the same day.

Even in the mid-fourth century BC, the Archaic temple (which, in keeping with many other temples of Artemis, faced west) had been one of the largest and most decorated buildings in the Greek world. One of the first marble temples, it was enfolded in a double row of columns, while a deep porch (whose ceiling was itself supported by two rows of columns) led to tall doors which in turn opened out into the *cella*, where a smaller inner sanctuary housed the cult statue. For mainland Greeks both *cella* and statue would have provoked curiosity. The first because it was roofless – its great width meant that it could not be spanned by rafters, and the architects had no wish to clutter it with columns. The second because at Ephesus Artemis was shown not as a lithe virgin huntress, but, inspired by Cybele, the Anatolian deity with whom she was identified, as an enigmatic fertility goddess clad in flowing robes decorated with images of animals and zodiacal signs, a tall crown on her head, and across her chest a multitude of oval objects, which have been variously interpreted as breasts, eggs, grapes and severed testicles.

Undeterred by their loss, the Ephesians resolved to build their new temple on an even grander scale. Despite its marshy location just outside the city, they set about constructing it above the old foundations to a similar design, albeit enlarging and raising the stylobate so that, now measuring 130 × 69 m

Opposite: A second-century AD statue of Ephesian Artemis shows a multitude of ovoids at her chest beneath zodiacal signs, while her dress and headdress are studded with animals.

Right: A marble column drum from the Hellenistic Temple of Artemis at Ephesus is sculpted with a mythological scene perhaps showing Alcestis being led to the Underworld.

Below: Lion-head spouts like this one channelled water from the roof of the Temple of Artemis at Ephesus.

Overleaf: This computer model of the Temple of Artemis at Ephesus suggests the building's scale and majesty. The goddess's statue can be seen through the open doors.

(425 × 225 ft), it stood on a ten-stepped platform, 4.8 m (16 ft) tall, and packing the substructure with fleeces and charcoal to act as seismic insulation. On this they raised a forest of 127 Ionic columns soaring 18 m (60 ft) in height, two rows round the back and sides, three at the front, with three further columns supporting the now open *opisthodomos*, and a double colonnade supporting the front (western) porch. The square bases and lowest drums of thirty-six of these (most likely the twenty-eight external columns on the west side, together with the eight in the west porch) were carved with sculptures, including one by the master sculptor Scopas. Their scale was daunting. Each sculpted block was more than 1.8 m (6 ft) tall and, were they to be unrolled and laid out flat, they would have stretched for more than half a kilometre (a third of a mile). Most are now lost, but fragments suggest that the high-relief bases contained scenes showing rapid movement, while the shallower carved drums were more static. Their subjects included the deeds of Theseus and Heracles, the Centauromachy and the Gigantomachy, as well as Nereids astride sea monsters, Victories leading sheep and cattle to be sacrificed, and perhaps

Alcestis, the Greek heroine who died (and rose again) for love of her husband, being led to the Underworld by Hermes.

Further sculptures adorned the entablature and pediments: creeping acanthus leaves and lion-head waterspouts, which seem so like those on the nearby Mausoleum at Halicarnassus that they may well be the work of the same sculptors, and when all this work was painted and gilded the effect must have been both dazzling and daunting. Meanwhile, the treasures which the building housed, including celebrated paintings and already venerated sculptures by old masters, were so numerous that Pliny, whose description of the temple is at best confused, does not even try to list them. 'There are', he writes, 'enough to take up many books'. More eloquent was the second-century BC poet Antipater, who gushed: 'I have gazed on the high walls of Babylon, atop which chariots can drive, and on Zeus' statue at Olympia. I have seen the hanging gardens, Rhodes' Colossus of the sun, the great works of the mighty pyramids and the towering Mausoleum. But when I looked at Artemis' temple, rising to the clouds, those other wonders faded, and I said: "Except for Mount Olympus, there is no other sight beneath the sun that can compare."'

No wonder Alexander wanted to be part of it. In 334 BC, following his first great victory over the Persians at Granicus, he passed through Ephesus and, finding the temple under construction, offered to pay for its completion. This put the Ephesians in a quandary. The Archaic temple had been part-funded by Lydia's King Croesus, who had gone on to be defeated by the Persians. Who could tell that Alexander would not share his fate, and, if he did, how would the Persians treat them if they accepted money from the Macedonian? So, they came up with a clever, fawning answer. It would be wrong, they said, for one god to make a dedication to another.

The people of nearby Priene were less fastidious. Set on the terraced slopes of Mount Mycale, and backed by towering cliffs, Priene looked across a busy bay towards Miletus, destroyed by the Persians at the end of the Ionian Revolt but now a resurgent Persian-leaning city. But threatening the prosperity of all the local seaside towns were alluvial deposits from the River Maeander, which were causing the bay to silt so rapidly that by the mid-fourth century BC the old settlement of Priene, which once stood at the river mouth, was already some distance from the coast. So, perhaps encouraged the satraps of Halicarnassus, the Prieneians moved further west to found a city, whose grid pattern followed the

'EXCEPT FOR MOUNT OLYMPUS, THERE IS NO OTHER SIGHT BENEATH THE SUN THAT CAN COMPARE.'

ANTIPATER

Alcestis, the Greek heroine who died (and rose again) for love of her husband, being led to the Underworld by Hermes.

Further sculptures adorned the entablature and pediments: creeping acanthus leaves and lion-head waterspouts, which seem so like those on the nearby Mausoleum at Halicarnassus that they may well be the work of the same sculptors, and when all this work was painted and gilded the effect must have been both dazzling and daunting. Meanwhile, the treasures which the building housed, including celebrated paintings and already venerated sculptures by old masters, were so numerous that Pliny, whose description of the temple is at best confused, does not even try to list them. 'There are', he writes, 'enough to take up many books'. More eloquent was the second-century BC poet Antipater, who gushed: 'I have gazed on the high walls of Babylon, atop which chariots can drive, and on Zeus' statue at Olympia. I have seen the hanging gardens, Rhodes' Colossus of the sun, the great works of the mighty pyramids and the towering Mausoleum. But when I looked at Artemis' temple, rising to the clouds, those other wonders faded, and I said: "Except for Mount Olympus, there is no other sight beneath the sun that can compare."'

No wonder Alexander wanted to be part of it. In 334 BC, following his first great victory over the Persians at Granicus, he passed through Ephesus and, finding the temple under construction, offered to pay for its completion. This put the Ephesians in a quandary. The Archaic temple had been part-funded by Lydia's King Croesus, who had gone on to be defeated by the Persians. Who could tell that Alexander would not share his fate, and, if he did, how would the Persians treat them if they accepted money from the Macedonian? So, they came up with a clever, fawning answer. It would be wrong, they said, for one god to make a dedication to another.

The people of nearby Priene were less fastidious. Set on the terraced slopes of Mount Mycale, and backed by towering cliffs, Priene looked across a busy bay towards Miletus, destroyed by the Persians at the end of the Ionian Revolt but now a resurgent Persian-leaning city. But threatening the prosperity of all the local seaside towns were alluvial deposits from the River Maeander, which were causing the bay to silt so rapidly that by the mid-fourth century BC the old settlement of Priene, which once stood at the river mouth, was already some distance from the coast. So, perhaps encouraged the satraps of Halicarnassus, the Prieneians moved further west to found a city, whose grid pattern followed the

'EXCEPT FOR MOUNT OLYMPUS, THERE IS NO OTHER SIGHT BENEATH THE SUN THAT CAN COMPARE.'

ANTIPATER

On the terraced slopes of Mount Mycale, the Temple of Athena Polias at Priene once looked across the wide Bay of Miletus.

precepts of the local fifth-century town planner Hippodamus of Miletus.

The **Temple of Athena Polias at Priene** stood near city's highest point on a broad terrace commanding a magnificent sea view. Designed by Pythius, the Mausoleum's architect, its proportions were meticulously planned. Measuring from the axis of the corner columns, its length, 37 m (122 ft), is exactly twice that of its breadth, while the width of each of the square column plinths, 1.8 m (6 ft), matches exactly the distance between them. Indeed, the entire building was designed on a grid, its pattern accentuated by paving stones set round the *sekos* and inside both the square porch and the shallow *opisthodomos*. Some architectural elements are borrowed from the Mausoleum, such as the square plinths of the Ionic columns which rose almost 11.5 m (38 ft) tall and were topped by capitals whose design and execution were virtually identical to the

Above: A marble block from Priene's temple wall bears the inscription: 'King Alexander dedicated this temple to Athena Polias'.

Opposite: This marble head, possibly of Alexander's ally, Queen Ada, was discovered in the *cella* of the Temple of Athena Polias.

Mausoleum's. Similarly, too, the ceiling between architrave and *sekos* was studded by coffers, twenty-six in all, and carved in low relief, within 'lids' just over 0.6 m (2 ft) square. The only figurative sculptures on the entire building, these were similar in style to the Mausoleum's Amazonomachy, but here their subject was the Gigantomachy, whose gods included Anatolian Cybele, holding a drum in her left hand while she rides, side-saddle, on a lion which mauls a stricken giant. Even the coffer showing Athena is alive with Asiatic influences, bringing with them a greater exuberance and ornate extravagance than was seen in Classical Greek art; in a departure from earlier depictions of the giant Enceladus, her fallen foe, being run through by her spear, has sprouted wings and writhing, snaky legs.

By the time of Alexander's visit around 334 BC, most of these coffers seem to have been set in place and, perhaps encouraged by his recent victory and in the hope of more to come, the Prieneians used the occasion of their liberation from the Persians to identify their temple as a second Parthenon, that is, a memorial to Persian defeat. They did this by installing as cult statue a half-sized replica of Pheidias' Athena Parthenos with winged Victory alighting on her outstretched palm. But, instead of being chryselephantine, this was a cut-price copy, its exposed flesh made in marble and all the rest being gilded metal covering an armature of wood. Even the plinth was hollow, faced with a thin marble façade. Most likely, Alexander never saw it, but he ordered an inscription to be set up on the temple in recognition

of his help in funding it: 'Alexander dedicated this temple to Athena Polias.' Meanwhile, the notion of a Parthenon set up in Asia to mark his crushing of the Persians captured his imagination, and towards the end of his short life he was planning such a temple at Troy.

A century later, his dream became reality. In the 230s BC, Hellenistic workmen levelled much of the Trojan acropolis (destroying Bronze and Iron Age remains in the process) and on a massive terrace raised a marble colonnaded temple, 35.6 m (117 ft) long and 16.4 m (54 ft) wide, the arrangement of whose cycle of metopes deliberately mirrored the Parthenon's, with the Trojan War facing north, the Gigantomachy east, the Centauromachy south and the Amazonomachy east. The best surviving slab shows Helios the sun god in his four-horse chariot, his features redolent of those of Alexander and his head encircled by a radiating halo, whose design is reminiscent of the sunburst emblem of Macedon's royal house.

For Alexander and his contemporaries, the ongoing east–west struggles between Greeks and Persians whose origins (they thought) lay in the Trojan War were visceral and raw. Nowhere could this be seen more clearly than at the **Temple of Apollo at Didyma** across the bay from Priene. Lying slightly inland some 18 km (11 miles) south of Miletus, to which it was linked by a Sacred Way flanked by seated statues, Didyma was Miletus' most holy site, home to a grove of laurel trees and a spring whose waters were believed to have prophetic powers. In the Archaic Age, a huge temple housed the god's cult statue, but in the dying days of the Ionian Revolt, the Persians torched the building and removed the statue to their royal palace at Ecbatana. For some time, as Didyma lost its former status, even the sacred spring dried up – until Alexander swept south to 'liberate' Miletus following a hard-won siege, when miraculously (so it was said) the waters bubbled up again, proclaiming to the world that Alexander truly was the son of Zeus. Not unsurprisingly, this pleased the conqueror, who ordered the rebuilding of the temple, and, following his defeat of Persia, returned the old cult statue to its home.

However, it was only after Alexander's death in 323 BC – when, following long campaigns that led him into India, he

Above: Inspired by a metope on Athens' Parthenon, one of the metopes of the Hellenistic Temple of Athena at Troy showed Helios, the sun god, his features perhaps inspired by Alexander, his halo reminiscent of the symbol of the Macedonian royal house, driving a four-horse chariot.

Opposite: This over-life-sized statue of a local prince was dedicated to Apollo at Didyma around 565 BC.

Overleaf: The scale of the Temple of Apollo at Didyma, imagined here in the second century AD, can be seen from the throngs of worshippers crowding its steps and portico.

succumbed to fever on his return to Babylon – that Seleucus, one of his successors, appointed two architects, Daphnis and Paeonius, to oversee the new construction. Theirs was a vision on a colossal scale. The substructure alone was huge. More than 5,481 sq. m (59,000 sq. ft) in area, the podium was almost 5.4 m (18 ft) in height, its seven steps (Apollo's sacred number) too high for worshippers to climb, so that the eastern side was furnished with a broad fourteen-stepped stairway. Around the stylobate there ran a double colonnade, 108 Ionic pillars (their bases carved with leaves and vegetation) each more than 2.4 m (8 ft) in diameter and 19.5 m (64 ft) tall, which carried an entablature from whose frieze stared a row of gorgon heads, and an elaborately coffered ceiling. A deep porch with three rows of four columns led to the great central double doors – but with

their threshold set 1.5 m (5 ft) above floor level these were clearly never meant for human worshippers to enter. Instead, unusually, they were flanked on either side by two small doorways from which narrow vaulted passageways sloped downwards to ground level and out into the *cella*, where an unwitting visitor would almost certainly have paused before a truly unexpected sight.

Unroofed, unpaved, its towering walls decorated with a frieze of griffins and studded with a forest of pilasters, their bases level with the porch, their tops carved with more painted griffins and unfurling foliage, the *cella* housed Apollo's sacred spring and laurel grove, an arboretum of well-tended trees luxuriating in their own protected microclimate. At the far side of this garden stood a further building. Rising on a shallow three-stepped base, 8.2 m (27 ft) wide and almost 14 m (47 ft) long, with four Ionic columns at the front, this was a discrete shrine, a temple in a temple, home to the recently returned cult statue. From here, looking back again beyond the trees, the

Below: Unroofed, unpaved and approached via narrow passageways, the *cella* of the Temple of Apollo at Didyma contained a sacred spring and olive grove as well as a chapel.

Opposite: The capitals of the Temple of Apollo's pilasters were decorated with winged griffins and unfurling vegetation.

visitor would have discovered further architectural innovations to explore. For at the east end of the *cella* was a monumental staircase, a flight of twenty-four steps 15 m (50 ft) in width that led up to a large chamber, whose floor level matched the height of the great double doors' raised threshold and whose ceiling was supported by two columns. The purpose of this room is now unknown, but even more perplexing are doors on either side of it that access claustrophobic stairways running up between the chamber and the *cella*'s outer walls. Since these are not preserved to their original height, it is impossible to know whether they once accessed the roof, or, if not, what their function was. They are so narrow that they must be climbed in single file, so did worshippers ascend by one set and descend by the other? And, if so, what happened when they reached the top?

Didyma's Temple of Apollo saw traditional Greek architecture approached with new dynamic creativity in terms of not just scale but also ingenuity, a hallmark of the Hellenistic Age, when, thanks to Alexander's conquests, more Greeks travelled more frequently in what had been the Persian Empire, becoming more familiar with its art and architecture. But these were uncertain times. Following Alexander's death, his empire was divided between his strongest, most ruthless lieutenants, many of whom founded dynasties whose feuding plunged the

Greek world into endless wars. In 305 BC, Demetrius, the son of one of Alexander's generals, laid siege to Rhodes (another grid-planned city, founded just over a century before to unify the island's population). However, aided by allies including Ptolemy I of Egypt (another of Alexander's generals), the Rhodians resisted, and Demetrius withdrew leaving many of his innovative siege engines and towers behind. Following an oracle's advice, the citizens of Rhodes began to worship Ptolemy as a god, dedicating to him a sanctuary, a square grove surrounded on all sides by stoas. Meanwhile, for their patron deity, the sun god Helios, they set up a statue.

The **Colossus of Rhodes** was a paean to the early Hellenistic Greek obsession with pushing the limits of technology to create a monument which for its sheer size and flamboyance would have been unthinkable a century before. That it was a failed experiment – it toppled in an earthquake, snapped at the knees fifty-four years after it was raised – does not detract from its ambition or ingenuity and it rightly earned its place as one of the seven wonders of the ancient world. Although nothing now remains and even its exact location is unknown, descriptions by Philo of Byzantium, who may have seen it while it stood, and the elder Pliny, who marvelled at its ruins, help us reconstruct it partially in the imagination.

From a base of white marble, the bronze figure of Helios soared above the entrance to Rhodes' harbour, 36.5 m (120 ft) in total height, the god's identity immediately apparent from the halo-crown of rays that emanated from his head. The brainchild of the sculptor Chares of Lindos, a city on the east coast of the island, it was funded from the sale or melting down of Demetrius' abandoned siege engines and weaponry, and it called for a radical new means of construction. Work began in 292 BC, and according to Philo (who perhaps consulted members of its construction team), the statue was erected layer on layer 'from earth to heaven', with each component moulded *in situ* before being cast in bronze to fit onto the part below. Built round a sturdy inner iron scaffolding, these bronze casts formed a hollow shell, infilled for stability with squared-off blocks of stone. However, since even these constituent parts were too heavy to winch into place, and given the statue's height, another method of construction needed to be found. So, they employed a technique familiar from sieges. As Philo explains, 'they constructed a huge earthen mound around the finished parts, covering the completed sections under the ground, and working on the next stage as they stood on the flat surface of

Top: A silver tetradrachm (four-drachma) coin from 289–288 BC shows a youthful Demetrius wearing the royal diadem of Macedon with bull's horns sprouting from his head to show his affiliation to the god, Dionysus.

Above: Ptolemy I of Egypt's portrait appears on this gold pentadrachm (five-drachma) coin minted in Cyprus. Like Demetrius, Ptolemy boasts a luxuriant head of hair, its style carefully curated to resemble Alexander's (see p. 200) to suggest the legitimacy of their succession.

Below: One of Demetrius' siege engines, the *helepolis* ('city-taker') is imagined in this French engraving from 1727.

Overleaf: The Colossus of Rhodes, a towering statue of the sun god, Helios, is imagined standing on a pedestal at the entrance to the city's commercial port.

what was underneath'. Twelve years after it was started, the great mound was removed and the finished statue revealed, shining in glory, 'a god', rhapsodizes Philo, 'equal to the god himself, a work superlative in daring, a second Helios to face the first.'

The Colossus' appearance can only be imagined, but, given the use of the mound and Philo's mention of a singular marble base as well as other technical considerations, it cannot have spanned the harbour mouth. Verses preserved in the *Greek Anthology*, however, tell how it dominated both the land and sea, so a site near the harbour is most likely. After the earthquake, its shattered pieces lay strewn across the ground, themselves a cause of wonder. More than two centuries later, Pliny the Elder marvelled at them, their 'vast yawning cavities' still filled with stones. 'Few men', he observed, 'can encircle its thumb with their arms', adding that while 'its fingers are larger than most statues ... there are a hundred other massive statues in this city, any one of which, though smaller, would have brought it fame.'

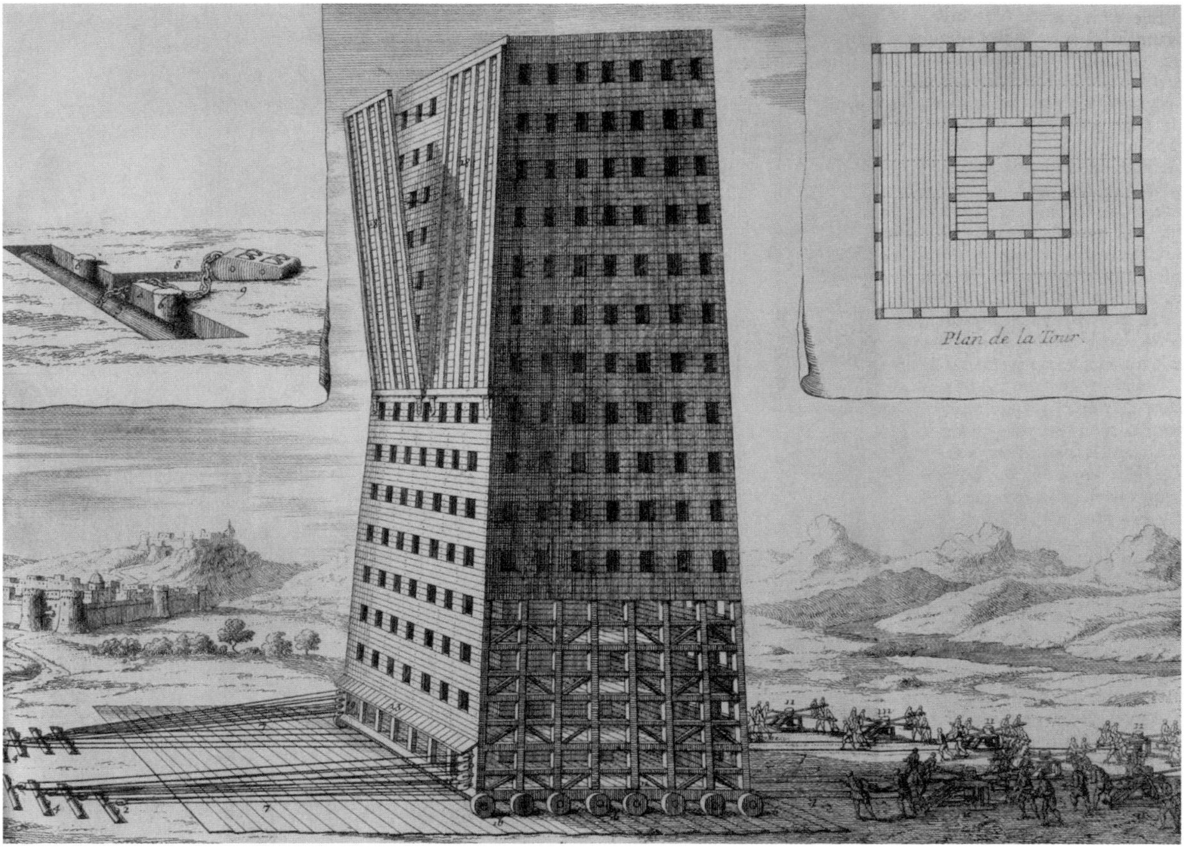

'A GOD EQUAL TO THE GOD HIMSELF ... A SECOND HELIOS TO FACE THE FIRST.'

PHILO
*On the Seven Wonders of the World*

Colossal artworks and impressive buildings were becoming *de rigueur*, with many of them still retaining some connection to religion. Such was the case at Pergamum, the wealthy city on a rocky outcrop that at well over a thousand feet dominated a well-watered plain in western Anatolia. Inhabited since at least the eighth century BC, Pergamum rose to prominence in the third century when Philetaerus, general to one of Alexander's successors, ringed its acropolis with massive walls, which were in turn expanded in the early second century to take in the entire hill where the rapidly expanding city stood. But Pergamum was not immune from either the wars of Alexander's successors or invasions by Celtic tribes, whom Greeks called Gauls, and who in 277 BC even managed to loot Didyma. However, Pergamum's kings were skilled tacticians and, despite being swept up in the maelstrom, the city thrived and grew to be a beacon of Greek culture.

Pergamum's kings enjoyed close ties with Athens, now more a leading cultural centre than a military superpower, and they fashioned their capital in that city's image, complete with its own Temple of Athena Polias (housing a copy of Pheidias' Athena Parthenos), whose axis was deliberately skewed to face the south so that it stood (like the Parthenon) above a Theatre of Dionysus (albeit one with an alarmingly steep auditorium). But their most striking monument was the so-called **GREAT ALTAR OF ZEUS**. Set on a huge terrace south of Athena's temple, and overhanging the theatre where it could be seen for many miles,

Above: Painted in 1570, Louis de Caullery's fanciful reconstruction of the Colossus wrongly imagines it straddling the entrance to Rhodes' harbour.

Opposite: A modern reconstruction shows the Great Altar of Zeus on its huge terrace at Pergamum.

Opposite: Today located in Berlin's Pergamon Museum, the reliefs of the Great Altar of Zeus are sculpted with great confidence in the new Hellenistic style.

Below: This second-century BC copy of Pheidias' statue of Athena from Athens' Parthenon was discovered in the library area near Pergamum's Temple of Athena.

this was one of the most innovative structures of its time. Begun around 165 BC by Eumenes II to celebrate his victories over the Gauls, the altar stood in its own courtyard on a raised platform approached from the west by a monumental staircase of twenty-four steps, 20 m (66 ft) wide. But most impressive was the structure on which the altar itself stood, for rising from a five-stepped base – just over 36 m (117 ft) wide and almost 33.5 m (110 ft) deep – to a height of 12 m (40 ft) was a marble podium, a slightly elongated square, whose wings embraced the staircase. At the level of the inner courtyard it was surrounded on three sides by an Ionic colonnade, whose marble roof was decorated lavishly with statues of gods, sea deities and rearing centaurs.

Around the podium's walls beneath the colonnade (in contravention of all earlier convention) there ran a frieze, 113 m (371 ft) long and 2.2 m (7 ½ ft) tall, its subject, the Gigantomachy, now serving as a metaphor for Pergamum's victory over the Gauls. It also paid homage to Athens' Parthenon, since Pergamum's Athena had precisely the same pose as Athena on the Parthenon's west pediment, its Zeus mirrored Poseidon from the same composition, and serpents similar to those carved on the Parthenon slithered up beside the stairway. But the frieze was no slavish copy. Sculpted with great confidence in high relief, painted so that its figures pulsated in the shifting light, it was imbued with the new Hellenistic style, its chunky bodies and its crowded detail so baroque as to be almost camp.

This was not the altar's only frieze. Around the courtyard's three inner sides, this time conventionally part of the entablature, another Ionic frieze, 1.5 m (5 ft) in height, showed the life of Telephus, a legendary Greek who moved to Asia, was involved in the early stages of the Trojan War and became Pergamum's founding hero. Much about the composition was innovative, not least that episodes from the same story were arranged in sequence to present a narrative, or the elements that showed where scenes were set, vegetation heralding a rural backdrop, architectural details anchoring the action indoors. There may have been an even stronger link between Telephus and the altar complex. Preserved in the foundations were remains of an earlier building, a tomb shrine similar to that of Hyacinthus at Amyclae, almost certainly once dedicated to Telephus.

Another of Pergamum's jewels gleamed in the agora behind the altar. Containing a wealth of manuscript rolls, many tens of thousands neatly tagged and pigeonholed, its library ranked among the largest in the world, matched only by that of its great

rival, Alexandria, the city founded by Alexander himself in 331 BC at one of the Nile's western mouths, now arguably the greatest urban centre in the entire Greek world. Laid out on a grid plan by the court architect Dinocrates (whose previous plan to turn Mount Athos in the north Aegean into a gigantic statue of a seated figure holding an entire city in his outstretched hand had come to nothing), Alexandria boasted two harbours, wide boulevards and residential areas divided into zones, each housing residents of different classes or ethnicities. It boasted, too, a royal palace with squares and colonnades that covered many acres; a library, its myriad manuscripts meticulously catalogued, a home to poets and intellectuals; and a museum (literally a Temple of the Muses), which was both a study centre for the leading scientists of the day– doctors, astronomers, inventors – and a repository for living specimens of plants and animals. And on a low island, linked to the mainland by a

Above: Athena destroys the giant Alcyoneus in a detail of the sculptures showing the Gigantomachy on Pergamum's Great Altar of Zeus.

Opposite: From the inner frieze of the courtyard of the Great Altar, a detail shows an episode from the life of Pergamum's founding hero Telephus.

causeway 1.2 km (¾ mile) long, was a lighthouse, so unequalled in efficiency and size that by the fourth century AD it was accepted as a wonder of the world.

Commissioned by Ptolemy I (Alexander's general who, on the conqueror's death, laid claim not to just Egypt but to Alexander's corpse before himself being worshipped as a god), the lighthouse, named for the island on which it stood, the **Pharos of Alexandria**, was begun shortly after 305 BC and completed under his son Ptolemy II's rule some twelve years later. At between 107 and 133 m (350 and 435 ft) tall and built from a white local stone, which gleamed like marble, it was the tallest building of antiquity. It had three distinct sections: the

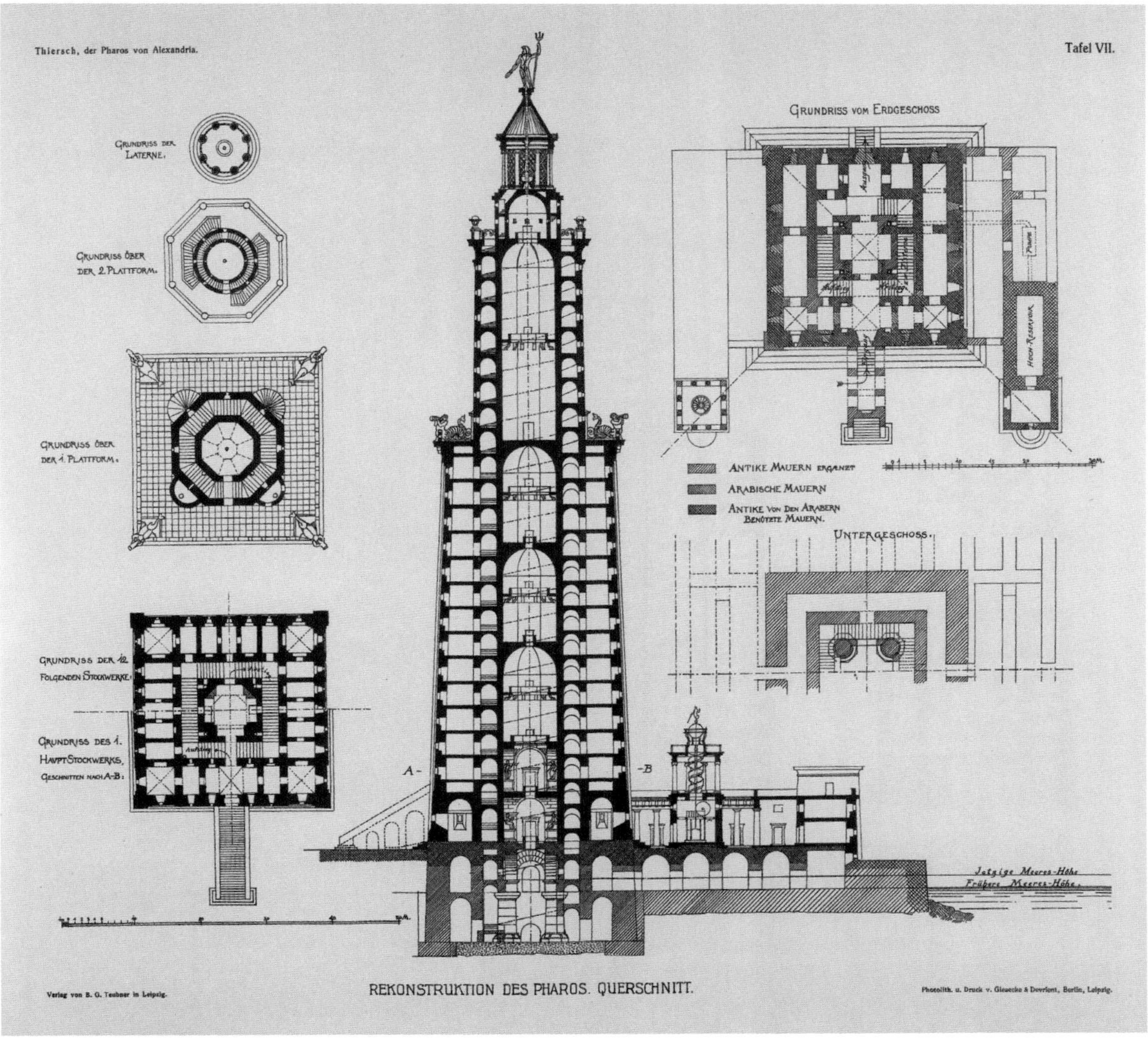


Opposite: Sited on an island at the entrance to Alexandria's great harbour, the Pharos was equipped with a huge convex bronze mirror which amplified firelight by night and the sun's rays by day.

Above: Based equally on description and speculation, this 1909 study by Hermann Thiersch presents one possible interior reconstruction of the Pharos of Alexandria.

lowest was square, 30m (100 ft) on each side tapering to 26 m (86 ft); the middle octagonal, 16.4 m (54 ft) across; and the upper cylindrical 8.8 m (29 ft) in diameter. While the two lower levels contained openings to dissipate the impact of high winds, the roof of the top section was supported by four columns, ringed by bronze statues of winds or sea gods and crowned with a bronze statue of Zeus (which may also have served as a weathervane). It was this highest level that contained the fire whose light was amplified across the sea at night by a huge convex bronze mirror, which also reflected the sun's rays by day, guiding sailors towards port and away from the deadly reefs and sandbanks of its neighbouring shores. The light was so dazzling that it could be seen 'like a second sun ... apparently suspended over the waters' (as the Roman novelist Achilles Tatius wrote) some 55 km (34 miles) out to sea. 'All night', enthused an earlier Greek poet, 'sailors carried by the waves will see the bright flame flashing from its top and will not go astray.'

During the night, however, no ship tried to enter harbour, but lay at anchor until morning, when the sunlight striking the Pharos' white walls picked out the bronze inscription: 'Sostratus of Cnidus ... to the Divine Saviours for those who sail at sea'. Sostratus was the architect, while the Divine Saviours' identity was deliberately ambiguous: were they the Dioscuri (the Heavenly Twins believed to protect mariners) or the Ptolemies and their sister-wives (since Egyptian royalty were worshipped in their lives as gods) or were they both sets of divinities? As pilots guided heavy-laden merchant ships to the wharf-lined waterfront, the lighthouse personnel would already be preparing for the coming night. A ramp ran up inside the building, wide enough for two mules to pass and fringed with entrances to storage rooms. Among equipment kept here must have been the fuel that kept the beacon burning, but what this was is now unknown. Most likely it was papyrus.

The wealth and elegance of Alexandria meant that the city was a jewel in the crown of the Greek world, while the fecundity of Egypt, now administrated by Greek-speaking civil servants who were every bit as bureaucratic as their Mycenaean ancestors, attracted the envy both of Greeks and of their western neighbour Rome. After victories over the Carthaginians, the Macedonians and Greeks, in 146 BC a Roman army swept into Corinth, unleashed carnage and destruction and removed priceless artworks back to Italy. Thirteen years later, rather than

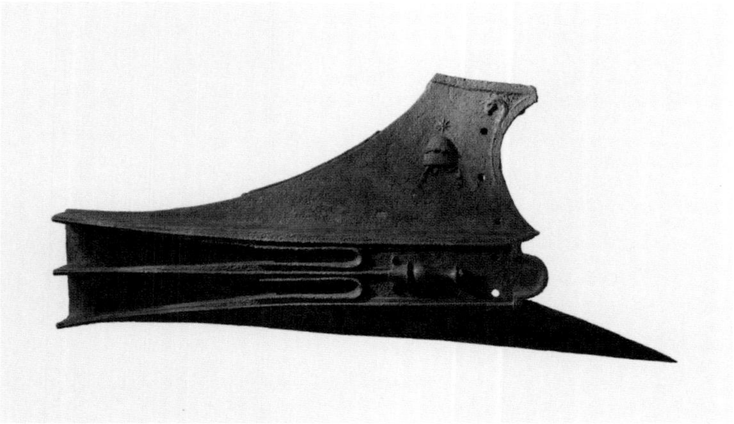

Left: Discovered off the coast of Israel, this three-pronged ram, one of the largest single bronze-castings known from antiquity, dates to the second century BC and was fixed to the prow of a warship.

Opposite: A modern reconstruction shows the retaining wall of the Victory Monument at Actium, studded with captured ships' rams and bearing an inscription commemorating Augustus' 'victory in the war waged for the Roman state'.

SPOLIIS·EXORNATA·CONSACRAVIT·VACAT·

see it pillaged, King Attalus III bequeathed Pergamum to the Roman senate and people. In the following decades Rome's grasp on Greece grew tighter, while its brutal civil wars spilled over into once-Greek territory. Some tried to resist – in vain. In 86 BC, Rome's general Sulla swept into Athens and its streets flowed with blood. By 44 BC Roman quinqueremes patrolled most of the Mediterranean, while legionaries occupied its hinterlands. Only Egypt remained independent (at least in name), but in the wake of the assassination of the dictator Julius Caesar even it was dragged into Rome's psychodrama. At last, in 31 BC, ships of its queen Cleopatra VII and her ally, the erstwhile Roman strongman but now increasingly deluded Marcus Antonius, were defeated by the fleet of their arch-rival Octavian (later Augustus) off the west of mainland Greece at Actium. The next year Alexandria, and with it Egypt, fell. The entire Greek world was now in thrall to Rome.

However, one monument remained to be erected, a monument that served as a transition between the architecture

of the independent Greeks and that of their new Roman masters, who would go on to plunder many of their ideas. It was the **Victory Monument at Actium**, commissioned by the now omnipotent Octavian. Although his admiral, Agrippa, had led his fleet to victory in waters just outside the wide Ambracian Gulf, Octavian chose to site the complex on a hillside a little to the north, from where he himself watched the battle from his camp. Built over two terraces, it combined religious piety with raw triumphalism. On the upper level stood a stoa, 'pi-shaped' like Pergamum's Altar of Zeus, 38 m (125 ft) long on every side, with a double colonnade – open to the south with views, beyond a row of trees, over the bay. In the centre of the square thus formed, on a platform 21.9 m (72 ft) long and 6.4 m (21 ft) deep, there rose an altar dedicated to Apollo, Octavian's patron god. Its sides were adorned with sculptures showing parts of warships and armour and weapons artistically arranged as trophies. On the upper register was an Ionic frieze, its subject a procession, but, unlike the processions carved on Ephesus' Temple of Artemis or on the Parthenon at Athens, here were shown not worshippers at an annual festival. Instead, they were victorious Romans leading not just captives but floats containing booty and wrecked warships, while on a four-horse chariot their godlike commander rode through the streets of Rome in triumph. There may have been another set of carvings, too, whose theme

Above: A first-century AD wall painting from the Temple of Isis in Pompeii shows two Roman warships rowing out of port.

Right: Set within the Victory Monument, a semi-cylindrical marble altar was carved with a procession of gods. Here Artemis leads a deer, while her mother Leto and the messenger god Hermes follow her.

Overleaf: Augustus erected the Victory Monument with its altar on the hillside from which he had watched his fleet destroy the ships of Marcus Antonius and Cleopatra at Actium in 31 BC.

·VACAT·IMP·CAESAR·DIVI·IULI·F·VICTORIAM·CONSECUTUS·BELLO·

displayed a bitter sense of irony, since there is evidence of an Amazonomachy, the battle against foreign women that once symbolised Greek victory over barbarians, co-opted now by Romans to celebrate their victory over a Greek-speaking Macedonian: Cleopatra.

The lower level of the monument made this victory quite literally tangible, for, below the upper terrace and built into its retaining wall, 63 m (206 ft) long and 7.3 m (24 ft) high, were thirty-six stone blocks, into each of which was fixed the bronze ram of a warship salvaged from the wrecks of Cleopatra and Antonius' fleet. Arranged by size, the largest to the west, the smallest to the east, and likely representing every class of ship in the defeated navy, they were accompanied by an inscription carved into smooth limestone in the victors' language, Latin. Using Octavian's then title 'Caesar', his rank '*imperator*' (then meaning 'general' but soon to embrace 'emperor') and the Latin names for Ares and Poseidon, it read: 'Imperator Caesar, son of Divine Julius, victor in the war he waged here for the Roman

Below: Carved during Augustus' reign (27 BC–14 AD) this sculpture from his triumphal arch at Arausio (Orange) in southern France shows a riot of rams and warships' prows.

Opposite, above: Dating from 14–37 AD, this marble relief originally from Praeneste (Palestrina) near Rome illustrates the Battle of Actium and the triumph of Augustus.

Opposite, below: This cameo from around 27 BC was created to commemorate Rome's victory at Actium and shows Augustus in a chariot being conveyed across the waves by sea gods.

state ... established peace here on both land and sea, dedicating to Mars and Neptune the camp whence he attacked the enemy, adorned now with ships' spoils.'

Meanwhile, across the bay on the promontory of Actium that gave the victory its name, a short way from where his enemy had camped near swamps for long malarial months before the battle, Octavian expanded an older Temple of Apollo, equipping it with monumental statues of the god and his twin, Artemis (whom Romans called Diana), and in a specially constructed exhibition space he displayed ten captured warships. Furthermore, on land sloping to the shore beneath his victory monument he founded a new city adorned with a fine theatre and stadium. Here he would celebrate four-yearly games to mark his conquest of the east, in a Roman town populated both by families summarily relocated from the region and by their undisputed conquerors, which, with a shameless lack of sensitivity, he named in Greek: Nikopolis, 'City of Victory'.

EPILOGUE

# AFTERLIFE

SHORTLY AFTER IT WAS BUILT, the exhibition space at Actium erected by Octavian (or Augustus as he soon let his subjects call him) burned down together with the warships it contained. Today, his victory memorial, too, lies in ruins, inaccessible behind high fences, while fronting the museum of Nikopolis, the tagline, 'one sea battle, one city, one empire' appears in Greek and English but not Latin.

As we have seen, the Actium monument showed many Greek influences, and the influence of Greek art and architecture came to dominate the Roman world and in turn influence Renaissance and later art and architecture across the entire world. As the Roman poet Horace observed, 'captured Greece captured her savage conqueror'. Thucydides' reflections, too, about how future visitors to ruined cities would be misled concerning their respective power, have stood the test of time, but only partially. To explore even the ruins of many of the monuments we have examined in this book is to experience a sense of wonder, not least at the ambitious confidence of those who built them or designed them or commissioned them, Greeks eager to embody abstract visions of their world within a physical reality.

Only four of our monuments are so completely lost that reconstructions must rely as much upon a mix of written evidence and informed guesswork as on archaeology or observation: Apollo's Throne at Amyclae, whose ultimate fate remains unknown, and the Colossus of Rhodes, the Pharos of Alexandria, and the Mausoleum of Halicarnassus, all of them victims of earthquakes, their constituent parts repurposed, their metal melted down, their dressed stone reused for breakwaters or (in the Mausoleum's case) a medieval castle. Natural disaster played its part elsewhere as well, though seldom on the scale seen at Thera, whose eruption destroyed most of the island and buried the West House and Xeste 3, beneath thick clouds of ash and pumice. More than two millennia later, at Olympia, a sixth-century AD earthquake toppled the now-abandoned and fire-damaged Temple of Zeus, collapsing its columns and smashing its sculptures. By then, the statue it had once contained, Pheidias' chryselephantine masterpiece, had also been destroyed. Dismantled, it had been transported to the Roman Empire's eastern capital, Constantinople, where flames engulfed its new home, a eunuch's palace, and it was lost forever. A similar fate may have befallen the same sculptor's Athena Parthenos. Constantinople became home to Delphi's Serpent Column, too, which was erected in the city's hippodrome, where

## 'CAPTURED GREECE CAPTURED HER SAVAGE CONQUEROR'

HORACE
*Epistles*

it remained intact until the seventeenth century. Today its stump still stands beside a busy street, while a replica of its fractured base has been set up at Delphi near six reconstructed columns of the Temple of Apollo, which itself was rebuilt following an earthquake in 330 BC.

For many temples equally destructive was the advent of Christianity and, with it, late-fourth-century AD decrees that put an end to pagan worship. Abandoned, most sank into disrepair, their materials a useful quarry for projects that at the time seemed more important than their preservation. As recently as the mid-eighteenth century, blocks from the great Temple of Zeus at Acragas were carted off to nearby Porto Empedocle to build a harbour wall. Some temples were more fortunate. In Syracuse, the Temple of Athena was repurposed as a cathedral, where its marble columns still stride down the nave and glow embedded in the outer walls. Athens' Hephaesteion, too, survived almost intact because of its conversion to a church, while the Parthenon experienced a plethora of metamorphoses as its fate mirrored that of mainland Greece, becoming a Cathedral of the Virgin Mary, then a mosque and then a store for dynamite, until in 1687 it suffered a direct hit from a mortar shell, exploded and became the ruins that, so carefully curated over many generations, now symbolize the civilization of not just Periclean Athens but the entire ancient Greek world. For actor and activist, Melina Mercouri, they were 'a monument that represents the national spirit of Greece', and her campaign to reclaim the Parthenon 'marbles' from London's British Museum contributed to a vexed ongoing debate surrounding the significance and ownership of relocated monumental objects.

Surprisingly, however, the remnants of many of our monuments still stand in their original landscapes. The Palace of Knossos, where peacocks strut and call through concrete reconstructions of plazas and paintings reimagined by Sir Arthur Evans in the early twentieth century, still sprawls on a fertile plain beneath Mount Iuktas' once-sacred summit; the Walls of Troy still ripple round its citadel, although the great bay that it once commanded is now silted up; in Sparta from the Menelaion the sun can still be seen to set behind the pyramidical high peak of Mount Taygetus; lion replicas still crouch above the sacred lake of Delos and replicas of caryatids still gaze out across the wreckage of the temple burned by Persians towards the Parthenon. Some monuments, such as Epidaurus' *tholos* and Philip's Palace at Aegae, have been recently restored. All that remains of others, such as the Siphnian Treasury at Delphi, the

Argive Heraion, even the Temple of Artemis at Ephesus, are their foundations and a scattering of sculptures in museums. Indeed, the Temple of Artemis, once a wonder of the world, was lost completely until a nineteenth-century engineer drawing on Roman inscriptions and his own determination found fallen columns in a swampy hollow near Selçuk, while the entire site of Olympia was only rediscovered in the eighteenth century.

Yet the ghost of every monument remains, as does the legacy of those who made them, and thanks to modern archaeologists, architects and artists we can begin to recreate them whether physically or in our own minds' eye. And as we do, we gain a sharper picture of what motivated those who first erected them – piety perhaps or patriotism, egotism, an urge to impress contemporaries or leave a mark for future generations – a complex web of motivations which can seem very modern. This re-animation of antiquity obsessed a Greek poet from Alexandria at the turn of the twentieth century AD. Constantine Cavafy's *Ionikon* expresses the idea perfectly (though for 'Ionia' we should perhaps, read 'Greece'):

*Just because we've smashed their statues,*
*just because we've chased them from their temples,*
*it does not mean the gods are dead at all.*
*Land of Ionia, they love you still,*
*their souls still hold your memory.*
*When an August sunrise dawns upon you*
*your atmosphere vibrates with life;*
*and sometimes a figure, young, ethereal*
*and indistinct, with swift foot*
*strides over your hills.*

In his 1868 painting *Phidias Showing the Frieze of the Parthenon to his Friends*, Lawrence Alma-Tadema imagines the artist displaying his freshly painted sculptures to Pericles along with Pericles' wife, Aspasia, and ward, Alcibiades. In fact, by the time the frieze was completed, Pheidias had already left Athens to create the statue of Zeus at Olympia.

# MAP

1. West House
2. Palace at Knossos
3. Palace at Phaistos
4. Fortress Citadel at Mycenae
5. Treasury of Atreus
6. Citadel of Tiryns
7. Walls of Troy
8. Palace at Pylos
9. Cult Areas at Troy
10. Menelaion
11. Lefkandi Heroön
12. Temple of Artemis at Corcyra
13. Temple of Apollo at Corinth
14. Tunnel of Eupalinus
15. Siphnian Treasury
16. Temple of Apollo at Delphi
17. Throne of Apollo
18. Temple of Hera at Olympia
19. Terrace of Lions
20. Theatre at Thorikos
21. Statue of the Tyrannicides
22. Soros
23. Athenian Treasury at Delphi
24. Serpent Column
25. Temple of Zeus at Acragas
26. Temple of Athena at Syracuse
27. Temple of Aphaea
28. Temple of Zeus at Olympia
29. Parthenon
30. Hephaesteion
31. Telesterion at Eleusis
32. Propylaea
33. Erechtheum
34. Temple of Athena Nike
35. Heraion of Argos
36. Temple of Apollo Epikourios at Bassae
37. Asclepium at Epidaurus
38. Tholos of Delphi
39. Mausoleum at Halicarnassus
40. Palace at Aegae
41. Lion of Chaeronea
42. Philippeion
43. Royal Necropolis at Aegae
44. Temple of Artemis at Ephesus
45. Temple of Athena Polias at Priene
46. Temple of Apollo at Didyma
47. Colossus of Rhodes
48. Great Altar of Zeus
49. Pharos of Alexandria
50. Victory Monument at Actium

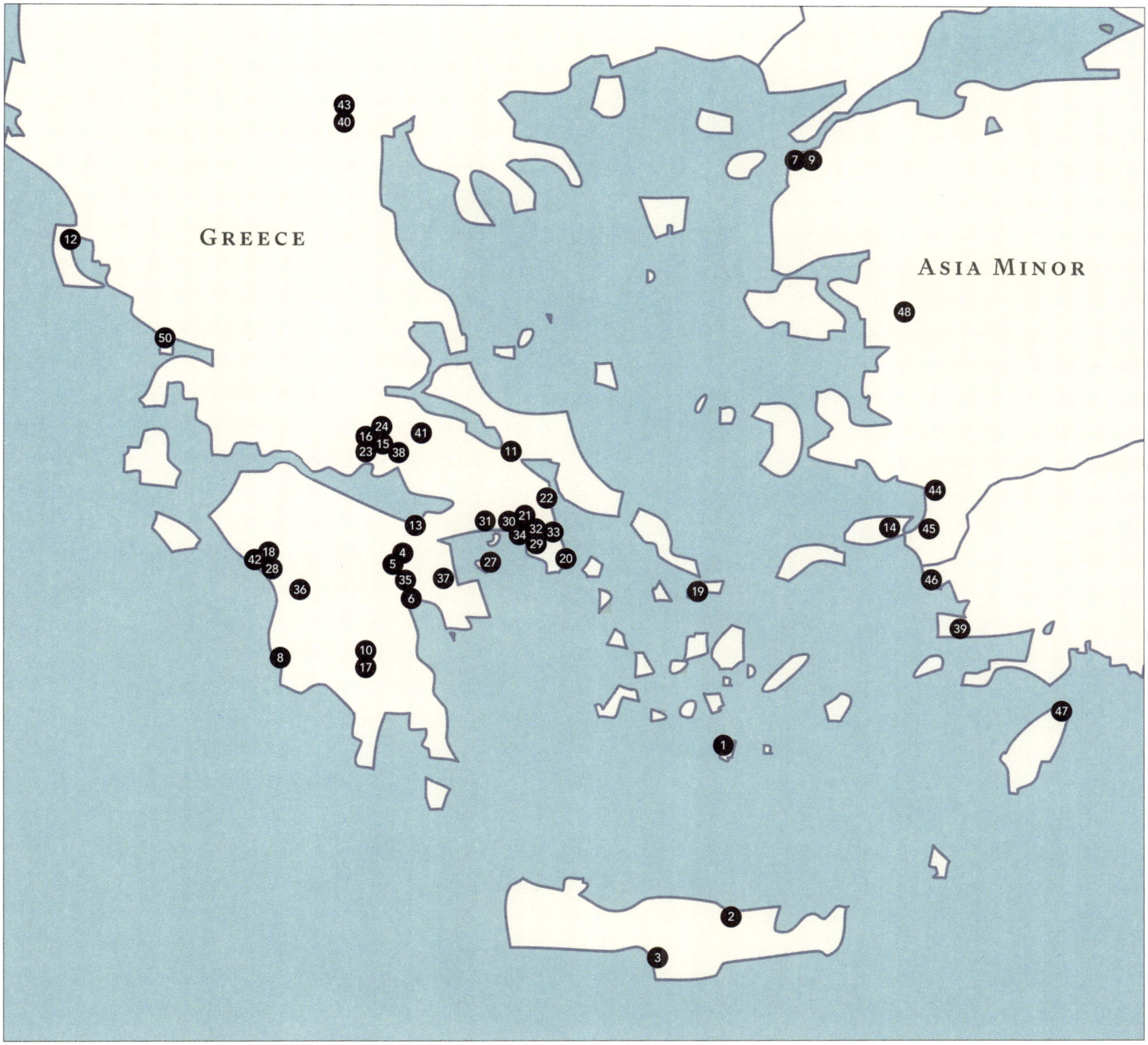
GREECE
ASIA MINOR
1
2
3
4
5
6
7
8
9
10
11
12
13
14
15
16
17
18
19
20
21
22
23
24
27
28
29
30
31
32
33
34
35
36
37
38
39
40
41
42
43
44
45
46
47
48
50

SICILY
25
26

EGYPT
49

# FURTHER READING


Barringer, Judith M. and François Lissarrague (eds), *Images at the Crossroads* (Edinburgh University Press, 2022)

Barringer, Judith M., *Olympia* (Princeton University Press, 2021)

Boardman, John, *The Art and Architecture of Ancient Greece* (London and New York: Thames & Hudson, 1967)

Bugh, Glenn R. (ed.), *The Cambridge Companion to the Hellenistic World* (Cambridge University Press, 2006)

Camp, John M., *The Athenian Agora* (London and New York: Thames & Hudson, 1986)

Cartledge, Paul, *Ancient Greece, A History in Eleven Cities* (Oxford University Press, 2009)

Cline, Eric H. (ed.), *The Oxford Handbook of the Mycenaean World* (Oxford University Press, 2010)

Hölscher, Tonio, *Visual Power in Ancient Greece and Rome* (University of California Press, 2018)

Hughes, Bettany, *The Seven Wonders of the Ancient World* (London: Weidenfeld & Nicolson, 2024)

Hurwitt, Jeffrey M., *The Athenian Acropolis* (Cambridge University Press, 1999)

Jenkins, Ian, *Greek Architecture and its Sculptures* (Cambridge, MA: Harvard University Press, 2006)

Lawrence, Arnold W., *Greek Architecture* (New Haven: Yale University Press, 1996)

Lyttelton, Margaret, *Baroque Architecture in Classical Art* (London and New York: Thames & Hudson, 1974)

MacEnroe, John C., *Architecture of Minoan Crete* (University of Texas Press, 2010)

Marconi, Clemente (ed.), *The Oxford Handbook of Greek and Roman Art and Architecture* (Oxford University Press, 2014)

Marinatos, Nanno and Robin Hägg, *Greek Sanctuaries* (London: Routledge, 1993)

Neer, Richard T., *Art and Architecture of the Greek World* (London and New York: Thames & Hudson, 2012)

Onians, John, *Art and Thought in the Hellenistic Age* (London and New York: Thames & Hudson, 1979)

Pollitt, Jerome J., *Art in the Hellenistic Age* (Cambridge University Press, 1986)

Romer, John and Elizabeth Romer, *The Seven Wonders of the World* (London: Weidenfeld & Nicolson, 2001)

Scott, Michael C., *Delphi* (Princeton University Press, 2014)

Shear, J. R., *Trophies of Victory* (Princeton University Press, 2016)

Spawforth, Tony, *The Complete Greek Temples* (London and New York: Thames & Hudson, 2006)

Steele, James and Ersin Alok, *Hellenistic Architecture in Asia Minor* (London: Academy Editions, 1992)

Stuttard, David, *A History of Ancient Greece in Fifty Lives* (London and New York: Thames & Hudson, 2014)

Stuttard, David, *Hubris: Pericles, the Parthenon and the Invention of Athens* (Cambridge, MA: Harvard University Press, 2026)

Tomlinson, Richard A., *Greek Architecture* (Bristol Classical Press, 1991)

Tomlinson, Richard A., *Greek Sanctuaries* (New York: St. Martin's Press, 1976)

## Sources of Quotations

All translations are the author's own.

Achilles Tatius, *Leucippe and Clitophon* 5.6 (p. 232)

Aeschylus, *Prometheus Bound* 798–801 (p. 61)

Antipater of Sidon, *Anth. Pal.* 9.58 (pp. 10, 210)

Constantine Cavafy, *Ionikon* (p. 244)

Diodorus Siculus, *Library* 13.82 (p. 122); 16.1 (p. 189)

Epictetus, *Discourses* 1.6 (pp. 10, 131)

Euripides, *Ion* 210–218 (p. 79)

Herodotus, *Histories* 8.144 (pp. 11, 86); 6.109 (p. 160)

Hesiod, *Works & Days* 145–151 (p. 16); 140–184 (p. 53)

Homer, *Iliad* 18.590–604 (p. 26); 11.173–177 (p. 33); 11.784 (p. 87); 1.266–268 (p. 134); *Odyssey* 8.63–64 (p. 49)

*Homeric Hymn to Apollo* 2–4 (p. 65); 146–155 (p. 89)

*Homeric Hymn to Dionysus* 11–12 (p. 94)

Horace, *Epistles* 2.1.156–157 (p. 242)

Justin, *Epitome* 9.3 (p. 197)

Lucian, *Dialogues of the Dead* 29 (pp. 185, 186)

Melina Mercouri, as quoted in *The Art Newspaper*, 10 May 2023 (p. 243)

Pausanias, *Description of Greece* 2.16.6 (p. 35); 3.19.2 (p. 84); 5.17.1 (p. 86); 8.41.8 (p. 168); 2.27.5 (p. 178); 9.40.10 (p. 189)

Philo, *On the Seven Wonders of the World* 4 (pp. 220, 224)

Pindar, *Pythian* 8.21–24 (p. 126)

Pliny, *Natural History* 36.4 (p. 184); 21.97 (p. 210); 36.21 (p. 221)

Plutarch *Life of Pericles* 13 (p. 10); fr. 178 (p. 148)

Posidippus, *Milan Papyrus* 115 (p. 232)

Simonides fr. 76 (Diehl) (p. 98); fr. 21 (Page) (pp. 106, 107)

Strabo, *Geography* 8.6.10 (pp. 164, 167)

Thucydides, *History of the Peloponnesian War* 1.10 (pp. 155, 163)

Vitruvius, *On Architecture* 7.12 (p. 182)

Xenophanes, fr. 15 (Diels–Kranz) (p. 92)

# SOURCES OF ILLUSTRATIONS

Listed by page number: a = above, b = below, l = left, r = right

Endpapers: From D. Le Roy, *Les ruines des plus beaux monuments de la Grece ...* (Paris, 1758). Getty Research Institute, Los Angeles

**2** From C. R. Cockerell, *The temples of Jupiter Panhellenius at Aegina...* (London, 1860). Heidelberg University Library, C 3260 Gross RES, p. 24_Plate_6_2; **6–7** © Jean-Claude Golvin; **8** Courtesy Ahmet Denker; **13** From A. C. Quatremère-de Quincy, *Le Jupiter olympien...* (Paris, 1815). Heidelberg University Library, 3236 A Gross RES, p. f; **14** Balage Balogh/ Archaeology Illustrated/akg-images; **16** Heritage Images/Fine Art Images/akg-images; **17** Photo Zdeněk Kratochvíl; **18**, 19a G. Dagli Orti/ DEA/De Agostini via Getty Images; **19b** © Carole Raddato/ followinghadrian.com; **20** © David Stuttard; **21a** Ashmolean Museum/ Bridgeman Images; **21b** © Carole Raddato/followinghadrian.com; **22–23** © JR Casals; **24** Erich Lessing/Bridgeman Images; **25** Photo Archaeological Museum of Heraklion (Π-Π1513 + 1524). © Hellenic Ministry of Culture/Hellenic Organization of Cultural Resources Development (H.O.C.RE.D.); **26** © Carole Raddato/followinghadrian.com; **27** Photo Archaeological Museum of Heraklion (**Π**5832). © Hellenic Ministry of Culture/Hellenic Organization of Cultural Resources Development (H.O.C.RE.D.); **28–29** Ralf Adler/ imageBROKER/Getty Images; **30** © Thames & Hudson Ltd; **30–31** Balage Balogh/Archaeology Illustrated/akg-images; **32** A. Garozzo/ DEA/DeAgostini via Getty Images; **33** Luisa Ricciarini/Bridgeman Images; **34** MYC/3/2/35, Mycenae Excavation Records, Archives. Reproduced with the Permission of the British School at Athens; **35** Balage Balogh/Archaeology Illustrated/akg-images; **36a** F. Scholz/ imageBROKER.com/Alamy; **36b** World History Archive/WHA/ akg-images; **37** G. Dagli Orti/© NPL - DeA Picture Library/Bridgeman Images ; **38–39** Balage Balogh/Archaeology Illustrated/akg-images; **40** Photo 2026 Museum of Fine Arts, Boston. All rights reserved/ William Francis Warden Fund/Bridgeman Images; **41** gezmen/ Alamy; **42** The Trustees of the British Museum. All rights reserved; **43** © Jean-Claude Golvin; **44** © Thames & Hudson Ltd; **45** Photo D. Nakassis/K. Pluta. © The Pylos Tablets Digital Project, Palace of Nestor Excavations, Department of Classics, University of Cincinnati; **46** Photo J. Vanderpool. © Palace of Nestor Excavations, The Department of Classics, University of Cincinnati; **47** Balage Balogh/Archaeology Illustrated/akg-images; **48** Watercolour reconstruction by Piet de Jong. © The Department of Classics; University of Cincinnati; **50** Bridgeman Images; **52** Metropolitan Museum of Art, New York; Fletcher Fund, 1932 (acc. 32.11.1); **53a** The Trustees of the British Museum. All rights reserved; **53b** National Archaeological Museum, Athens; **54a** Gaertner/ Alamy; **54b** Troia slide, 18817. © The Department of Classics, University of Cincinnati; **55** Metropolitan Museum of Art, New York; Fletcher Fund, 1956 (acc. 56.171.18); **56** Mark Landon (Wikimedia Commons/ CC-BY-4.0); **57** BSA SPHS/1/2941.7755, Sparta Excavation, BSA SPHS Image Collection, Archives. Reproduced with the Permission of the British School at Athens; **58** After J. Coulton. © Thames & Hudson; **59a** Archaeological Museum of Eretria/Ephorate of Antiquities of Euboea. © Hellenic Ministry of Culture/Hellenic Organization of Cultural Resources Development (H.O.C.RE.D.); **59b** DEA/DeAgostini via Getty Images; **60**, **61** Erich Lessing/akg-images; **62–63** Bridgeman Images; **64** From James Stuart and Nicholas Revett, *The Antiquities of Athens*, Vol. 3 (London, 1762). Getty Research Institute, Los Angeles; **65** Allard Pierson, University of Amsterdam, APM 2579; **66** Archivio J. Lange/DEA/DeAgostini via Getty Images; **67** Numismatic Museum, Athens; **69** Karol Kozlowski/robertharding/Alamy; **70a** Ioannis Tsouratzis/Alamy; **70b** Hercules Milas/Alamy; **71** © Thames & Hudson Ltd; **72–73** © Emiralikokal/Dreamstime.com; **74** Joe Bird/Alamy; **75** Alessandro Avondo/Alamy; **76** Luisa Ricciarini/Bridgeman Images; **77** © John Burge; **78** Liebieghaus Skulpturensammlung, Frankfurt a. M, , Forschungsprojekt Polychromie, Frankfurt am Main. Photo Liebieghaus Skulpturensammlung, Frankfurt am Main - Vinzenz Brinkmann - Ulrike Koch-Brinkmann - ARTOTHEK; **79** © Egisto Sani; **80–81** Beaux-Arts de Paris, Dist. GrandPalaisRmn/image Beaux-arts de Paris; **82** © Nikolai Sorokin/Dreamstime.com; **83** G. Dagli Orti/DEA/De Agostini via Getty Images; **84** Classical Numismatic Group, LLC (cngcoins.com); **85** From A. C. Quatremère-de Quincy, *Le Jupiter olympien...* (Paris, 1815). Heidelberg University Library, C 3236 A Gross RES, p. 210a; **86** The J. Paul Getty Museum, Villa Collection, Malibu, California, 73.AE.135. Digital image courtesy of Getty's Open Content Program; **87** From E. Curtius, F. Adler (eds) *Olympia* (Berlin, 1896). Heidelberg University Library, C 3237-4 Grossfolio SK: 2, Tafel 84; **88** © Giannis Giannelos; **89a** From M. Quatremère de Quincy, *Le Jupiter olympien...* (Paris, 1815). Getty Research Institute, Los Angeles; **89b** Erich Lessing/akg-images; **90–91** G. Cozzi/DEA/De Agostini via Getty Images; **92–93** Beaux-Arts de Paris, Dist. GrandPalaisRmn/image Beaux-arts de Paris; **92b** Nimatallah/akg-images; **95** FotoGablitz/iStock.com; **96–97** Guven Ozdemir/iStock.com; **99** Martin von Wagner Museum der Universität Würzburg. Photo P. Neckermann; **100** Photo © Andrea Jemolo. All rights reserved 2026/Bridgeman Images; **101** Prisma Archivo/Alamy; **102** G. Dagli Orti/© NPL - DeA Picture Library/ Bridgeman Images ; **103a** The J. Paul Getty Museum, Villa Collection, Malibu, California, 74.AA.12. Digital image courtesy of Getty's Open

Content Program.; **103b** The J. Paul Getty Museum, Villa Collection, Malibu, California, 74.AA.12. Digital image courtesy of Getty's Open Content Program.; **104** Peter Connolly/akg-images; **106** The Trustees of the British Museum. All rights reserved; **107** © Znm/Dreamstime.com; **108–109** Yale Center for British Art, New Haven; Paul Mellon Fund; **110** National Museums Scotland/Bridgeman Images; **111** Stefano Politi Markovina/Alamy; **112** Luisa Ricciarini/Bridgeman Images; **113** Beaux-Arts de Paris, Dist. GrandPalaisRmn/image Beaux-arts de Paris; **114** Luisa Ricciarini/Bridgeman Images; **115** Tayfun Öner; **116–117** © 2025 Reconstruction of Delphi. John Goodinson. Scientific advisor: Elena Partida; **118** From James Stuart and Nicholas Revett, *The Antiquities of Athens* (London, 1830). Heidelberg University Library, C 3226 A Gross RES: 3-4, p. II_Plate_3; **119** 3D Virtual Reconstruction of the Valley of the Temples in Agrigento by ALTAIR4 MULTIMEDIA - altair4multimedia.it; **120** The Trustees of the British Museum. All rights reserved; **121** M. Leigheb/DEA/De Agostini via Getty Images; **122–123** Balage Balogh/Archaeology Illustrated/akg-images; **124** GrandPalaisRmn (musée du Louvre)/Photo Hervé Lewandowski/ Thierry Le Mage; **125** Marta Carenzi/Mondadori Portfolio via Getty Images; **127** bpk, Bildagentur für Kunst, Kultur und Geschichte, Berlin/ Scala, Florence; **128–129** Christos the Greek/Alamy; **130** From A. Blouet, A. Ravoisié (eds) *Expedition scientifique de Morée* (Paris, 1838). Heidelberg University Library, C 3230 Gross: 3, p. t_55; **132–133** Balage Balogh/ Archaeology Illustrated/akg-images; **135** Travelpix/Alamy; **136** Fine Art Images/Heritage Images/Alamy; **137** Juan de Lara (parthenon3d.com); **138–139** Beaux-Arts de Paris, Dist. GrandPalaisRmn/image Beaux-arts de Paris; **140a** © Thames & Hudson Ltd; **140b** Beaux-Arts de Paris, Dist. GrandPalaisRmn/image Beaux-arts de Paris; **141** The Trustees of the British Museum. All rights reserved; **142–143** Peter Connolly/akg-images; **145** © David Stuttard; **146** From James Stuart and Nicholas Revett, *The Antiquities of Athens*, Vol. 3 (London, 1762). Getty Research Institute, Los Angeles; **147** Kostas Pavlis/iStock.com; **149** Luisa Ricciarini/Bridgeman Images; **150** Peter Connolly/akg-images; **151** From James Stuart and Nicholas Revett, *The Antiquities of Athens*, Vol. 2 (London, 1762). Getty Research Institute, Los Angeles; **152–153** bpk, Bildagentur für Kunst, Kultur und Geschichte, Berlin/Scala, Florence; **154** DEA/DeAgostini via Getty Images; **156** © 2025 Reconstruction of the Erechtheion. John Goodinson. Scientific advisor: Alexandra Lesk; **157a** © Thames & Hudson Ltd; **157b** Luisa Ricciarini/Bridgeman Images; **158** © David Stuttard; **159l, 159r** From James Stuart and Nicholas Revett, *The Antiquities of Athens*, Vol. 2 (London, 1762). Getty Research Institute, Los Angeles; **160** © 2025 Reconstruction of the temple of Athena Nike. John Goodinson. Scientific advisor: Peter Schultz; **161** Luisa Ricciarini/Bridgeman Images; **162** The Trustees of the British Museum. All rights reserved; **163** Metropolitan Museum of Art, New York; Gilman Collection, Purchase, The Horace W. Goldsmith Foundation Gift, through Joyce and Robert Menschel, 2005, acc. 2005.100.1149; **164** G. Dagli Orti/DEA/De Agostini via Getty Images; **165** From C. Waldstein, *The Argive Heraeum* (Boston, 1902). Heidelberg University Library, C 3231-12, P6; **166** From A. C. Quatremère-de Quincy, *Le Jupiter olympien ...* (Paris, 1815). Heidelberg University Library, C 3236 A Gross RES, p. 326a; **167** © Carole Raddato/followinghadrian.com; **168** © John Bethell. All rights reserved 2026/Bridgeman Images; **169** From C. R. Cockerell, *The temples of Jupiter Panhellenius at Aegina...* (London, 1860). Heidelberg University Library, C 3260 Gross RES, p. 54_Plate_11; **170** The Trustees of the British Museum. All rights reserved; **171** © 2025 Reconstruction of the sanctuary of Asclepius at Epidaurus. John Goodinson. Scientific advisors: Peter Schultz. John Svolos; **172** © Gary Lee Todd; **173** G. Dagli Orti/DEA/De Agostini via Getty Images; **174–175** Stefanos Kyriazis/Alamy; **176** G. Dagli Orti/ DEA/De Agostini via Getty Images; **178** © Alexstreinu/Dreamstime.com ; **179** Archivio J. Lange/DEA/DeAgostini via Getty Images; **180–181** Balage Balogh/Archaeology Illustrated/akg-images; **183** © Jean-Claude Golvin; **184** The Trustees of the British Museum. All rights reserved; **186** Balage Balogh/Archaeology Illustrated/akg-images; **187a** DEA/DeAgostini via Getty Images; **187b** © Thames & Hudson Ltd; **188** © Egisto Sani; **190** Photo Polycentric Museum of Aigai/ Ephorate of Antiquities of Imathia. © Hellenic Ministry of Culture/ Hellenic Organization of Cultural Resources Development (H.O.C.RE.D.); **191** A. Dagli Orti/DEA/De Agostini via Getty Images; **192** Ullstein Bild/Getty Images; **193** From E. Curtius, F. Adler (eds) *Olympia* (Berlin, 1896). Heidelberg University Library, C 3237-4 Grossfolio SK: 2, Tafel 119; **194–195** © Jean-Claude Golvin; **196** From E. Curtius, F. Adler (eds) *Olympia* (Berlin, 1896). Heidelberg University Library, C 3237-4 Grossfolio SK: 2, Tafel 79; **197** The Trustees of the British Museum. All rights reserved; **198** © Jean-Claude Golvin; **200** The Trustees of the British Museum. All rights reserved; **201** © Konstantinos Lagos/Dreamstime; **202** Michael Runkel/robertharding/ Alamy; **203** DEA/DeAgostini via Getty Images; **204** A. Dagli Orti/DEA/ De Agostini via Getty Images; **205** Rijksmuseum, Amsterdam; **206** Nicholas Saunders/akg-images; **207a, 207b** The Trustees of the British Museum. All rights reserved; **208–209** Courtesy Ahmet Denker; **211** © Egisto Sani; **212, 213** The Trustees of the British Museum. All rights reserved; **214** bpk, Bildagentur für Kunst, Kultur und Geschichte, Berlin/ Scala, Florence; **215** The Trustees of the British Museum. All rights reserved; **216–217** Balage Balogh/Archaeology Illustrated/akg-images; **218** © Selcuk Oner/Dreamstime; **219** Manuel Cohen/Scala, Florence; **220a** Metropolitan Museum of Art, New York; Gift of C. Ruxton Love Jr., 1967, acc. 67.265.30; **220b** Art Institute of Chicago; Gift of Martin A. Ryerson, acc. 1922.4933; **221** Universal History Archive/Universal Images Group via Getty Images; **222–223** © Jean-Claude Golvin; **224** GrandPalaisRmn (musée du Louvre)/Photo Tony Querrec; **225** © 2025 Reconstruction of Pergamon. John Goodinson; **226** Erich Lessing/ akg-images; **227** bpk, Bildagentur für Kunst, Kultur und Geschichte, Berlin/Scala, Florence; **228** Erich Lessing/akg-images; **229** E. Lessing/ DEA/De Agostini via Getty Images; **230** © Jean-Claude Golvin; **231** From H. Thiersch, *Pharos* (Leipzig, Berlin, 1909). Heidelberg University Library, C 5388-7 Folio, Tafel 7; **232** Photo © William M. Murray; **233** Reconstruction by Mr. Fotis Tsakmakis. Image courtesy Dr. Konstantinos Zachos. Ephorate of Antiquities of Preveza. © Hellenic Ministry of Culture/Hellenic Organization of Cultural Resources Development (H.O.C.RE.D.); **234–235** Samuel Magal/Alamy; **235** Photo Archaeological Museum of Nicopolis (AMN 01097)/ Ephorate of Antiquities of Preveza. © Hellenic Ministry of Culture/ Hellenic Organization of Cultural Resources Development; **236–237** Reconstruction by Mr. Fotis Tsakmakis. Image courtesy Dr. Konstantinos Zachos. Ephorate of Antiquities of Preveza. © Hellenic Ministry of Culture/Hellenic Organization of Cultural Resources Development (H.O.C.RE.D.); **238, 239a** © Carole Raddato/ followinghadrian.com; **239b** DEA/DeAgostini via Getty Images; **240, 245** Photos Birmingham Museums Trust, licensed under CC0

# INDEX

Page numbers in *italic* refer to illustrations

*For my wife, Emily Jane, and my mother, Kate.*

ACKNOWLEDGMENTS

Monuments must be commissioned. So, too, must books, and I feel greatly honoured to have been invited to write this book by Ben Hayes, Commissioning Editor at Thames & Hudson, to whom my first thanks go. It has been a pleasure to work with him and Associate Editor India Jackson once again. It has been a pleasure, too, to work for the first time with my editor, Emma Barton, and picture researcher Pauline Hubner. Their contribution to this book cannot be exaggerated. My thanks, too, to all those who have been involved with its layout, production and marketing. As with any building project, the bringing of a book to fruition requires a large team of specialists, and the team at Thames & Hudson has (as always) been exemplary.

Thank you to all those with whom I have travelled the Mediterranean, either privately or more recently with Noble Caledonia, to visit most of the monuments covered here, from well preserved temples to 'heaps of rubble'. Their enthusiasm has been infectious and their observations thought provoking. I hope that they, as well as its other readers, will appreciate the many reconstructions that this book contains.

Last, and most profoundly, thank you to the home team: my mother, Kate, for her many years of support; my wife, Emily Jane, for her constant belief in me, and for the memorable journeys to antiquity that we have made together and will make again; and to our two cats, Stanley and Oliver, whose wisdom and devotion have earned them both – to quote the Roman poet Horace (as they themselves so often do) – a monument more lasting than bronze.

Frontispiece: C. R. Cockerell's 1860 reconstruction of the east façade of Aegina's Temple of Aphaea captures the vivid sense of movement in its pedimental sculptures.

Pages 6–7: A reconstruction of Delphi in the second century BC shows the Temple of Apollo and associated buildings on the slopes of Mount Parnassus, with the stadium top left and the Sanctuary of Athena Pronaia bottom right.

First published in the United Kingdom in 2026 by Thames & Hudson Ltd, 6–24 Britannia Street, London WC1X 9JD

First published in the United States of America in 2026 by Thames & Hudson Inc., 500 Fifth Avenue, New York, New York 10110



Cover designed by Daniele Roa



EU Authorized Representative: Interart S.A.R.L., 19 rue Charles Auray, 93500 Pantin, Paris, France
productsafety@thameshudson.co.uk
interart.fr

A CIP catalogue record for this book is available from the British Library

Library of Congress Control Number 2026935851

ISBN 978-0-500-02921-3
01

Printed in China by RR Donnelley

MIX
Paper | Supporting responsible forestry
FSC® C144853